Cambridge Elements ☰

Elements in Ethics
edited by
Ben Eggleston
University of Kansas
Dale E. Miller
Old Dominion University, Virginia

CONTEMPORARY VIRTUE ETHICS

Nancy E. Snow
The University of Oklahoma

CAMBRIDGE
UNIVERSITY PRESS

CAMBRIDGE
UNIVERSITY PRESS

University Printing House, Cambridge CB2 8BS, United Kingdom

One Liberty Plaza, 20th Floor, New York, NY 10006, USA

477 Williamstown Road, Port Melbourne, VIC 3207, Australia

314–321, 3rd Floor, Plot 3, Splendor Forum, Jasola District Centre,
New Delhi – 110025, India

79 Anson Road, #06–04/06, Singapore 079906

Cambridge University Press is part of the University of Cambridge.

It furthers the University's mission by disseminating knowledge in the pursuit of
education, learning, and research at the highest international levels of excellence.

www.cambridge.org
Information on this title: www.cambridge.org/9781108706339
DOI: 10.1017/9781108580496

First published 2020

A catalogue record for this publication is available from the British Library.

ISBN 978-1-108-70633-9 Paperback
ISSN 2516-4031 (online)
ISSN 2516-4023 (print)

Contemporary Virtue Ethics

Elements in Ethics

DOI: 10.1017/9781108580496
First published online: October 2020

Nancy E. Snow
The University of Oklahoma

Author for correspondence: Nancy Snow, nsnow@ou.edu

Abstract: This Element provides an overview of the central components of recent work in virtue ethics. The first section explores themes in neo-Aristotelian virtue ethics, while the second turns the discussion to major alternative theoretical perspectives. The third section focuses on two challenges to virtue ethics. The first challenge is the self-centeredness or egoism objection, which is the notion that certain kinds of virtue ethics are inadequate because they advocate a focus on the person's own virtue and flourishing at the expense of, or at least without due regard for, the concerns of others. The second consists of situationist challenges to the idea that there are indeed virtues and that personality is integrated enough to support virtues.

Keywords: virtue ethics, neo-Aristotelianism, situationism, self-centeredness objection

ISBNs: 9781108706339 (PB), 9781108580496 (OC)
ISSNs: 2516-4031 (online), 2516-4023 (print)

Contents

Introduction

How should I live? How should I act? What kind of person should I try to be? These and other questions are central to the field of ethics. The questions of how to live and what kind of person to be have an ancient pedigree, going back to the philosophers Plato, Aristotle, and the Stoics. They thought that these questions and others are best approached by thinking in terms of virtues – the kinds of characteristics a person should have in order to live a good life – qualities like courage, honesty, and generosity, to name but a few. In addition to being the key concept in the ethical theories of Plato, Aristotle, and the Stoics, virtue continued to be of interest to medieval philosophers such as St. Thomas Aquinas. It fell into abeyance, however, with the rise of modern philosophy and the emergence of deontology and consequentialism.

The past decades have seen a dramatic resurgence of interest in the ancient idea of virtue and of approaches to ethics in which the concept of virtue plays a central role. Any attempt to provide an overview of contemporary virtue ethics needs to be selective, since there is so much work being done in the field. Consequently, there is much that will of necessity be omitted from this account (such as religious virtue ethics and virtue ethics in non-Western traditions), but I will attempt to select topics from within contemporary Anglo-American virtue ethics, and its roots in Aristotle, that give a flavor of the ongoing interest and dynamism of the field, including its relevance to how we live our lives today.[1]

The origin of the present renewed interest in virtue is typically traced to a seminal article by Elizabeth Anscombe, "Modern Moral Philosophy" (1958). In this paper, Anscombe, who spent substantial periods of time at both Oxford and Cambridge, laments that neither deontology nor consequentialism provides an adequate philosophical psychology, and urges a return to Aristotle to fill this gap. Anscombe's general line of thought was continued in Oxford in the 1970s, by Peter Geach in *The Virtues* (1977) and Philippa Foot in a collection of essays, *Virtues and Vices and Other Essays in Moral Philosophy* (1978). Foot's thinking evolved and continued into the twenty-first century, with the publication of *Natural Goodness* (2001). Other philosophers on both sides of the Atlantic continued work on virtue, most notably Alasdair MacIntyre in *After Virtue: A Study in Moral Theory* (1984; originally published in 1981), *Dependent*

---

[1] Readers interested in religious virtue ethics are invited to consult the essays by Wood (2018), Vogler (2018), and Bucar (2018) for topical overviews of Christian and Islamic ethics; those by Sim (2018) and Tiwald (2018) for similar treatments of Confucianism, and by MacKenzie (2018) for Buddhism. Those who wish to delve more deeply should consult Nolan (2014), Austin (2018), and Dunnington (2019) for religious virtue ethics. Flanagan (2011) offers a naturalistic interpretation of Buddhism, and Stalnaker (2020), Slingerland (2011), Olberding (2012), Angle (2009), and Sim (2007) all furnish interesting perspectives on Confucianism.

Rational Animals: Why Human Beings Need the Virtues (1999), and *Ethics in the Conflicts of Modernity: An Essay on Desire, Practical Reasoning, and Narrative* (2016). Several papers by John McDowell have also contributed importantly to the literature on virtue, as have papers by Martha Nussbaum (1988), David Solomon (1988), Gary Watson (1990), and Bernard Williams' book *Ethics and the Limits of Philosophy* (1985).[2] Linda Zagzebski's work, *Virtues of the Mind: An Inquiry into the Nature of Virtue and the Ethical Foundations of Knowledge* (1996), unified a virtue-oriented approach to ethics with a similar approach to epistemology,[3] and was influential in developing what is known as 'responsibilist' virtue epistemology – a form of epistemology according to which knowledge is achieved through the possession of intellectual virtues such as open-mindedness, curiosity, perseverance, carefulness in inquiry, and so on. Thinking on virtue has also been buttressed by important works by scholars of ancient philosophy, such as Julia Annas' magisterial book on ancient ethics, *The Morality of Happiness* (1993).

The event that triggered the present deluge of books and articles on virtue, however, was the publication in 1999 of Rosalind Hursthouse's *On Virtue Ethics*. This was the first comprehensive attempt to put virtue ethics on the same theoretical footing as deontology and consequentialism. *On Virtue Ethics* is wide-ranging in scope, seeking, among other things, to show structural similarities among the three theory types; to answer the challenge that virtue ethics is incapable of giving action guidance by articulating a virtue ethical criterion for right action; to address the question of appropriate motivation; and to provide a foundation for virtue ethics in ethical naturalism. Hursthouse's book paved the way for the subsequent articulation of neo-Aristotelian virtue ethics, which is currently the most well-developed theoretical approach on offer.

I discuss central features of neo-Aristotelian virtue ethics in the first section of this *Element*. After giving a brief overview of key elements of Aristotle's theory, I pose a series of questions to focus and motivate the discussion. I then turn to alternative theoretical perspectives in Section 2. In Section 3, I focus on two central challenges to virtue ethics: the charge that virtue ethics is egoistic or self-centered, and situationist critiques, which apply mainly to neo-Aristotelian virtue ethics. I end this volume with brief concluding comments.

---

[2] Due to space constraints, I mention Nussbaum, Solomon, and Watson only in passing in later sections, and do not discuss Williams' or McDowell's contributions at all. Two seminal papers by the latter are McDowell (1979) and McDowell (1998).

[3] Epistemology is the area of philosophy that is concerned with questions such as how knowledge can be achieved, how to justify beliefs, whether skepticism (doubt about whether we can attain knowledge) is warranted, and so on.

1 Neo-Aristotelian Virtue Ethics

As the name suggests, neo-Aristotelian virtue ethics has been inspired by Aristotle's ethical theory. It has been developed most extensively by Alasdair MacIntyre in *After Virtue: A Study in Moral Theory* (1984; originally published in 1981), *Dependent Rational Animals: Why Human Beings Need the Virtues* (1999), and *Ethics in the Conflicts of Modernity: An Essay on Desire, Practical Reasoning, and Narrative* (2016); Rosalind Hursthouse in *On Virtue Ethics* (1999) and several papers; and Daniel C. Russell in *Practical Intelligence and the Virtues* (2009) and other work. After an overview of the central tenets of Aristotle's theory, I turn to central issues treated in the emergence and development of contemporary neo-Aristotelian virtue ethics, and conclude with ethical naturalism, the meta-ethical position which grounds many versions of it.[4]

1.1 Aristotle's Ethics in Brief

Aristotle is centrally concerned with what makes a life good – with what he calls *eudaimonia*.[5] This term is difficult to translate, but 'flourishing' seems to capture a good deal of Aristotle's meaning. We flourish when we live well, and we live well when our lives are infused with virtues. In other words, we live well when we live honestly, courageously, generously, and so on. To understand in more depth what this means for Aristotle, let's begin with the 'big picture.'

Aristotle believes that humans are part and parcel of a larger cosmos, and as such, we are members of one biological species among many others. Thus, he takes what is called a 'naturalistic' perspective by situating human beings as part of a larger physical and biological universe. We are distinguished from other animals by our capacity for reason. Aristotle's perspective is also teleological – as rational beings by nature, we are capable of thinking and of directing ourselves to our natural end, which is *eudaimonia*. Virtues, in the proper sense, are rational excellences that both contribute to and partially constitute human flourishing (see also Russell 2009). (Though Aristotle acknowledges virtues of thought as well as virtues of character or moral virtues, our discussion is confined to the latter.) To say that virtues are rational excellences is to say

---

[4] 'Meta-ethics' is the term used to refer to the theories that ground normative ethical positions, such as deontology, consequentialism, and virtue ethics. We will not encounter many meta-ethical positions in this Element – only neo-Aristotelian ethical naturalism (later in this section) and the sentimentalist meta-ethics proposed by Michael Slote (in Section 2).

[5] Eudaimonism, or efforts to understand the nature of the good life, is present in both ancient philosophy and, now, in contemporary virtue ethics. For an authoritative treatment of ancient eudaimonism, see Annas (1993). Contemporary accounts informed by ancient views include Russell (2012) and LeBar (2013). Baril (2014) and LeBar (2018) provide informative overviews. For contemporary non-Aristotelian accounts, see Besser-Jones (2014) and McMullin (2019). As with other topics of interest in virtue ethics, lack of space prevents me from exploring these views.

that they are informed by *phronēsis*, or practical wisdom. To get clearer on virtues as rational excellences, we should note that Aristotle contrasts them with what he calls 'natural virtues.' Natural virtues are not informed by practical wisdom. They are attributable to children whose rational capacities are not fully developed, and even to animals, as when we say, for example, 'the lion is courageous,' or 'the dog is loyal.' Lacking practical wisdom, natural virtues do not have the reliability that Aristotle ascribes to virtues as rational excellences. Without this reliability, natural virtues can contribute to human flourishing only by luck or chance. By contrast, virtues as rational excellences are the stable and controlling element in human flourishing. Flourishing, however, consists not only of virtue, but also of external goods, such as wealth, noble birth, friends, good children who have not died, and good looks. Today we might add food, shelter, clean water and air, and other goods that help us both during our formative years and later. Virtues as rational excellences cannot indemnify us against the possible misfortune of losing external goods, and thus cannot guarantee that we will flourish. However, virtues as rational excellences are our best bet for living a *eudaimon* life, for practical wisdom gives them stability, and thus, reliability (see Hursthouse 1999). They are entrenched dispositions of character that can see us through difficult times when we lose external goods or when they are at risk. Examples of Aristotelian moral virtues include some that are familiar to us and have already been mentioned, such as courage and generosity, and some that are less familiar or seemingly alien, such as wit, magnificence – the virtue that guides large expenditures for civic purposes – and magnanimity – the virtue of being, and knowing oneself to be, worthy of great honors.

Aristotle's definition of virtue, provided in Book II of the *Nicomachean Ethics*, is this: "Virtue is a state that decides, consisting in a mean, the mean relative to us, which is defined by reference to reason, i.e., to the reason by reference to which the intelligent person would define it. It is a mean between two vices, one of excess and one of deficiency" (*Nicomachean Ethics*, 1107a). To understand it fully, we need to refer to Aristotle's sparse remarks, also offered in Book II, on how virtue is developed.[6] We are not by nature virtuous or vicious, according to Aristotle, but instead, we have the capacity to become virtuous. We become virtuous through habituated action. If we have a proper upbringing, we will become habituated to perform virtuous action, and to take pleasure in doing virtuous things. Eventually, we will act virtuously not for the sake of the pleasure involved, but for the sake of doing the right thing; that is, we

---

[6] See also the *Nicomachean Ethics* on the role of the family and the state in cultivating virtue. Brief comments on habits and habituation can also be found in Aristotle's *Eudemian Ethics*, 201; 247.

will act virtuously because we see the value of virtuous action in its own right. How this is supposed to happen is a bit mysterious, but we can imagine a young person doing virtuous acts only because she has been told to do so or because she thinks they will bring her some material benefit or advantage. Consider that a college student might initially volunteer with the elderly at a nursing home only to get an entry on her resumé. Over the course of time, we can hope that she would become engaged by the activity, and would come to see the value of volunteering for its own sake. In doing so, she would be developing virtues such as compassion, benevolence, and generosity. She would be developing these traits through her repeated performance of actions, which though not truly virtuous at the beginning of her volunteer work, become so over the course of time.

Returning now to the definition, we can note that to be virtuous, our actions must be, at least initially, based on a choice or decision, which is in turn guided by reason, that is, *phronēsis*. Practical wisdom must guide virtuous action to ensure a measure of reliability in hitting the target of virtue. That is, practical wisdom enables us to be mostly successful in virtuous action, to hit the mark when we try to act compassionately or generously. We can hit the mark when we aim for the mean between two extremes, one of excess and one of deficiency. So, for example, courageous action is the mean between the excess of rashness and the deficiency of cowardice, and generosity, between the excess of profligacy and the deficiency of stinginess. Actions express and reinforce the character states from which they arise. Thus, it is important to be correct in our actions, and Aristotle gives practical advice in Book II on how to achieve the mean relative to us.

But humans are notoriously fallible in their capacities, and reason is no exception. Thus, the reasoning that guides virtuous action to a mean that is relative to us is set against the standard of the intelligent person – the *phronimos*. The concept of the *phronimos* is notoriously vague, but the idea to be taken from Aristotle's discussion is that we hit the targets of virtue in our actions, thereby achieving the mean, and, through repeated virtuous actions, develop entrenched virtuous character states, by fine-tuning our own capacities with reference to a higher standard. Thus, to use an idea from the work of Philippa Foot (1978), virtue functions as a kind of corrective to our own flawed tendencies. This is true both with respect to reason and to our motivational tendencies. Consider that, for Aristotle, virtue is the character state in which we know what the good is, desire to do the good, and act virtuously. Continence, by contrast, is the character state in which we know what the good is, do not desire to do it, but fight our desire, and do it anyway. Incontinence, or weakness of will, is the character state in which we know the good, do not want to do it, give in to our desire, and act viciously. Vice is the character state in which we do not know the real good, perhaps because we have mistaken an apparent good for the real good, do not desire to act in accordance with the real good but to act in accordance with an apparent good, and act viciously. To illustrate, if we are truly generous, we will give in the right way at the right time for the right reason. Our giving will be guided by practical wisdom, and done for the right reason – because it will benefit the other, or is the right thing to do in the circumstances. It will be appropriate in the circumstances, and will hit the target of virtue, being neither profligate nor stingy. Importantly, our giving will be done with the right emotion – wholeheartedly and open-handedly. By contrast, if we are continent, we could know that the right thing to do is to give generously, but not want to do it, or not want to do it for the right reasons. In such a case, we might give grudgingly, or only out of a desire to ingratiate ourselves with another. If we are weak of will, we will not give at all. If we are vicious, we might give because we are mistaken about what makes giving good – we might think, for example, that giving is good only because it is a tool to be used to try to gain control over others, and that is why we give.[7]

Before leaving Aristotle, two further points merit mention. First, like many other ancient ethicists, Aristotle holds a version of the 'unity of virtues' thesis. Plato holds this thesis in its strongest form: all virtues are forms of wisdom or knowledge – the knowledge of good and evil – and all form a unity. Aristotle does not hold the thesis in this strong form, but instead, maintains that virtues are unified in a weaker way: one cannot have any virtue unless one has them all. This thesis is related to our second point, namely, Aristotle's views on practical wisdom. Practical wisdom unifies the virtues. One cannot have practical wisdom without virtue, and one cannot have virtue without practical wisdom. Moreover, practical wisdom itself is unified: there is not a separate form of practical wisdom intrinsic to generosity and another to courage, for example (see Russell 2009). Practical wisdom has two roles: to guide specific virtues in the performance of right action, and to balance virtues among themselves, including adjudicating between them in cases of conflict. As we will see, contemporary neo-Aristotelians grapple with these themes: how to explain virtue ethical right action, how to think about conflicting virtues, and how to understand the unity of the virtues. Before turning to these topics, we must address the question, "Why virtue ethics in the first place?"

---

[7] Another interpretation of vice should be mentioned. According to this interpretation, the choice of vice is analogous to the choice of virtue. Since virtue is knowing the good and choosing it for its own sake, vice must be knowing the evil and choosing it for its own sake. Those who choose evil must also desire to act viciously, just as those who choose the good must desire to act virtuously. Thanks to a reviewer for making this point.

1.2 Why Virtue Ethics?

Virtue ethics, as conceived by Aristotle and continued in Christianized form by medieval philosophers such as St. Thomas Aquinas, sat comfortably within a world view that has been called 'Aristotelian-Thomistic.' A central aspect of this perspective is that it is strongly teleological – every element in the universe is directed toward attaining an end or *telos*. For Aristotle, the end for rational human beings is flourishing or *eudaimonia*, which is achieved through living a life of virtue supplemented by external goods. For Aquinas, the end of rational beings is the *summum bonum*, which consists both of earthly good and of unification with God at the end of time. The rise of science and the Enlightenment during the late seventeenth and eighteenth centuries upset the Aristotelian-Thomistic worldview, causing philosophers to abandon the strong sense of teleology at its core. Two new approaches to ethics were developed: deontology, championed by Immanuel Kant, and utilitarianism, defended by Jeremy Bentham and John Stuart Mill. These theory types, though very different in many respects, have a common structure: both take a moral principle as central, and attempt to derive guidance on how we should act by applying the principle to certain situations. For Kant, the central moral principle is the Categorical Imperative. Though it has many different forms, its most intuitively accessible version is the Means–Ends Formula: Always act so that you treat rational humanity, in yourself or in the person of another, always as an end and never as a means only. Applying that principle to situations allows us to discern our duties, and thus, how we should act. Should I lie to my parents about my grades? In lying, Kant would say, I treat my parents as a means to my end of hiding the truth, and thereby disrespect their rational humanity. Consequently, I have a duty to not lie. For Kant, the motive is what gives the action its moral worth: I must act from respect for the Moral Law (Categorical Imperative). Though utilitarianism has the same basic structure as Kantianism, the application of its central principle to situations can yield very different results from Kantian deontology. That central principle is the Principle of Utility. One familiar formulation is this: Always act so as to produce the greatest good for the greatest number of people. On this view, the consequences of an act (whether it brings about more happiness than available alternatives) determines its moral value. If lying to my parents about my grades would lead to the greatest good for the greatest number (would make me and my parents happy), then lying is morally permissible. There are many versions of both deontology and utilitarianism, but my central point is that they are similar in structure and furnish a decision procedure for deciding how I should act. That is, if I don't know what to do in any given situation, I can apply the Categorical

Imperative or the Principle of Utility, and generate an answer. Thus, both theories are well suited to providing action guidance. So why ask for more? Why turn, in the latter half of the twentieth century, back to virtue?

1.3 Initial Turns to Virtue

Of course, not all moral philosophers made the turn to virtue at this time. Deontology and utilitarianism are still alive and well. But others were not happy with these two theory types. As mentioned in the introduction of this Element, a seminal paper by Elizabeth Anscombe (1958) spurred the turn back to virtue by criticizing shortfalls of deontology and utilitarianism. Anscombe's concerns were quite serious. She argued that the moral concepts used in modern moral philosophy, such as 'ought' and 'obligation,' had become detached from earlier frameworks, such as Jewish, Christian, and Stoic ethics, that had made them intelligible. Unmoored from these frameworks, they become unintelligible and possibly, harmful (Anscombe 1958, 1, 6; see also van Hooft 2014, 2). Others in Oxford developed her line of thinking, but here I would like to note the pivotal role played by Alasdair MacIntyre's book, *After Virtue* (1981), in elaborating Anscombe's insights. Now in its third edition, on its publication the book stimulated tremendous interest in virtue as an alternative to modern ethical theories including deontology and utilitarianism. Though MacIntyre did not take the tack of developing virtue ethics as a comprehensive alternative theory type paralleling key aspects of deontology and utilitarianism – that did not occur until Hursthouse (1999) – his critiques of modern ethical theories arguably paved the way for that development.

His hypothesis in *After Virtue* is that the language of morality in the contemporary age is in grave disorder. He writes:

> What we possess, if this view is true, are the fragments of a conceptual scheme, parts which now lack those contexts from which their significance is derived. We possess indeed simulacra of morality, we continue to use many of the key expressions. But we have – very largely, if not entirely – lost our comprehension, both theoretical and practical, or [*sic*] morality. (MacIntyre 1984, 2)[8]

A way out of this malaise is available, and that is to return to the insights of the ancient Greeks and medievals about virtue. MacIntyre takes this path, arguing at length that virtues are the dispositions that sustain practices that are part and parcel of living traditions.[9] These practices occur in individual lives over time, which are lived in the context of families and communities. Individual lives

---

[8] All quotes from *After Virtue* are from the second (1984) edition.
[9] See MacIntyre (1984, chapter 15, especially 218ff) for an extensive discussion of these points.

possess narrative unity, that is, we can tell coherent stories about the lives of individuals, the virtues they possess, and how they exercise those virtues in ways that bring goods to their lives. Living traditions are those in which stories are passed on through generations. The goods that virtues bring are internal to the practices in which they are exercised and for which they are necessary; they should be contrasted with external goods, such as money. To illustrate, a certain kind of knowledge is an intrinsic good that is internal to academic practices, which are parts of academic traditions, and it is achieved through virtues such as curiosity, perseverance, the love of learning, a commitment to scholarship, and academic integrity. Someone who is not part of the practices and traditions of academia cannot achieve the good of knowledge in the same way as someone whose life is embedded in academic practices and communities. Most academics now receive salaries and stipends for speaking, reviewing manuscripts, and so on. But these payments are external to the practices of seeking and transmitting knowledge, and are not part of what makes the good achieved through practices intrinsically valuable. The virtues not only help us to sustain these practices, but also to ward off the temptations and dangers that might derail our efforts to live a good life. The good life for humans, MacIntyre (1984, 219) contends, is the life spent in seeking the good life; having and exercising the virtues help us to grow in knowledge of what the good truly is.

Despite the popularity of *After Virtue*, MacIntyre's and other efforts to revive interest in virtue encountered questions and criticisms. For example, doesn't the embeddedness of virtue in specific traditions and cultures entail moral relativism – the idea that there are no universal moral truths, but only moral truths that are specific to cultures and societies? Does the focus on the virtuous person imply a form of self-centeredness or egoism – that I should be concerned about *my* virtue, and not so much about the well-being of others? Finally, as already noted, given the main principles of deontology and utilitarianism and their ability to give clear action guidance, why turn to a view that seems to focus on individual character and away from the regulation of action?

Subsequent efforts to develop an ethics of virtue are found in important papers by Nussbaum (1988), who looks to Aristotle to develop a view of virtues as regulating spheres of human life and choice that are present in every culture or society, thereby countering the charge of moral relativism. Solomon (1988) describes versions of what an ethics of virtue might look like and tackles the self-centeredness objection. We will address another response to the relativism objection subsequently in this section, and revisit the self-centeredness objection in Section 3. For now, let us turn to the development of virtue ethical theory and the problem of virtue ethical right action.

1.4 Virtue Ethical Theory and Virtue Ethical Right Action

Some have complained that virtue ethics is incapable of giving action guidance –
a central function of ethical theories that critics claim is easily handled by
deontology and utilitarianism (see Louden 1984). By contrast, neo-
Aristotelian virtue ethics can supply only vague guidance, such as, "Do as the
phronimos would do." But this, critics say, does not tell us much.[10]

Enter Rosalind Hursthouse. In *On Virtue Ethics* (1999), Hursthouse aims to
put virtue ethics on the same theoretical footing as deontology and utilitarianism, including regarding its ability to give action guidance. She does this by
arguing that all three theory types share structural similarities. As with deontology and utilitarianism, she maintains that virtue ethics incorporates a criterion
of right action. That is, just as deontology and utilitarianism provide principles,
which, when applied to situations, give us guidance about how to act, so, too,
does virtue ethics.

Hursthouse's (1999, 28) criterion of virtue ethical right action is this: "An
action is right iff it is what a virtuous agent would characteristically (i.e., acting
in character) do in the circumstances." Crucial to her case that all three theory
types are structurally similar is that the central principles of deontology and
utilitarianism are, by themselves, incapable of providing action guidance. Each
requires explanation and supplementation. For example, utilitarians need to
explain what happiness is. Several accounts are on offer – happiness is pleasure
and the absence of pain, the maximization of the satisfaction of subjective
preferences, or some conception that combines objective and subjective elements of well-being. Deontological principles too, require explanation. Similarly,
Hursthouse believes that additional content is required if we look to the virtuous
person for action guidance, and we find it by looking to specific virtues.
Conceptions of bravery, honesty, and compassion give content to our ideas of
what the virtuous person would do in given situations. Additionally, central
principles are supplemented by 'rules of thumb,' such as 'Do not lie,' 'Do not
break promises,' and so on. Virtue ethics, Hursthouse claims, provides 'v-rules,'
which refer to the specific virtues to generate lists of prescriptions and prohib-
itions to guide right action. Would the truthful person lie if doing so is to her
advantage? Would she tell a hurtful truth with cruelty or compassion? Would the
generous person be stingy with her resources or give wholeheartedly and open-
handedly, and so on? Hursthouse admits that the v-rules often do not tell us

---

[10] It should be noted that some virtue ethicists do not think that virtue ethics has a problem with
right action (see, for example, Annas 2014; Chappell 2017). Yet, many others do, and the
problem has loomed large in the work of virtue ethicists who seek to develop virtue ethics as
a comprehensive theoretical alternative to deontology and utilitarianism. Consequently, I include
discussion of it here.

which specific action to perform in any given situation, that is, what the perfect gift is or how truthful one should be in a difficult situation. She maintains, however, that the same is true of the other theory types – often, we do not know exactly what to do to maximize happiness in any given situation, or what our duty in fact entails.

Hursthouse goes on to refine her criterion of virtue ethical right action, but we have enough information to get a basic idea of how she thinks that virtue ethics can provide action guidance: we are to act as the virtuous person would characteristically act in any given situation – with courage, charity, generosity, and so on. By her own admission, however, virtue ethics does not tell us exactly what to do in any given situation. If my Aunt Edna, for example, who is wearing a perfectly hideous hat, asks me how it looks, should I tell her the brutally honest truth, should I lie, or should I tactfully seek to evade the question? Perhaps deontology and utilitarianism could not give me action guidance in this case, but saying this is cold comfort when we turn to virtue ethics to help us to act well.

Hursthouse's view of the virtue ethical criterion of right action has been much criticized.[11] Indeed, there has been lively discussion in my classroom of how to respond to Aunt Edna's question, and it seems that practical wisdom might suggest many possible responses. Even in cases in which only a single virtue seems called for, Hursthouse does not take into account the fact that most of us are imperfectly virtuous, and are lacking in practical wisdom. We might not know how the virtuous person would characteristically act in any given situation, and might make mistakes because of our lack of knowledge. Suppose that a friend has lost his job. I want to help, and know that the virtuous person would act generously. I conclude that generosity requires that I give him money. On further reflection, however, it is not at all clear that this is what the virtuous person would or should do. The truly virtuous person would carefully consider all of the parameters involved – the fact that my friend has his pride, for example, and that giving him what he perceives to be a "handout" would wound it. The virtuous person might in fact opt for a different course of action, perhaps by giving him work in exchange for the money. The upshot is that our own shortfalls can prevent us from knowing what the virtuous person would do in some situations. But if so, Hursthouse's criterion hasn't given us very good action guidance.

Johnson (2003) makes one of the most interesting critiques by pointing out that mature but imperfectly virtuous agents might need to perform actions that a fully virtuous person, acting in character, would not need to do. He gives an example of someone who tends to lie in difficult situations. She seeks to break

---

[11] See, for example, Das (2003), Kawall (2009), and Johansson and Svensson (2018).

herself of this habit by keeping a journal, noting when she has lied or told the truth, as a way of keeping track of her progress in overcoming this flaw. From a virtue ethical perspective, this seems like the right thing to do. Yet it falls foul of Hursthouse's criterion. Johnson's critique is interesting not only for its contribution to the debate about virtue ethical right action, but also because it highlights the importance of virtue development – an issue we will take up later in this section.

For now, let us turn to a different question. If I need to know what the virtuous person would do in order to act virtuously, I need to know what the virtues are. So what are they? Is there a finite list of the virtues? To address these questions, we need to turn to another neo-Aristotelian philosopher, Daniel C. Russell.

1.5 Russell: The Enumeration Problem

Like Hursthouse, Russell (2009, xi) seeks to defend virtue ethics. He defends what he calls 'hard virtue ethics,' against 'soft virtue ethics.' Hard virtue ethics requires that every virtue be informed by practical wisdom; soft virtue ethics does not make this claim.[12] Russell (2009) offers an account of virtue ethical right action that requires that we know what all of the virtues are – that we be able to enumerate or list them. The enumeration problem is the problem of whether such a list exists, and how we can know it.

We will not go into the details of Russell's account of virtue ethical right action here, but will note its connection with the enumeration problem. Russell (2009, 44) argues that if virtue ethics is to give guidance about right actions, it must take into account all of our serious practical concerns. What this means, according to Russell, is that there must be a finite, specifiable list of virtues. Otherwise, if the list of virtues is infinite, the virtuous person will not be able to meet all of our serious practical concerns when deciding how to act, and thus, will not be able to perform virtue ethical right actions. To go back to the case of Aunt Edna's hat, if we are to stand any chance of deciding how to answer virtuously when she asks us whether it looks good, we must be able to take into account a range of practical concerns. One practical concern is our commitment to truth and honesty. Another is our concern not to hurt Aunt Edna's feelings. So far, it seems that honesty might conflict with compassion. Perhaps tact in expressing a difficult truth in a gentle way is in order. Thus a third virtue, that of tact, could be implicated. Other concerns and other virtues could arise. Perhaps Aunt Edna asks this question at a holiday gathering, and a truthful answer would spoil the occasion for everyone. The example shows that even in

---

[12] Proponents of various versions of 'soft virtue ethics' include Swanton (2003), Adams (2006), Slote (2001), and Driver (2001). See Russell (2009, xi).

a seemingly ordinary situation, numerous virtues could be called for. To act rightly, according to Russell, we must meet all of the practical concerns that arise in the situation, and this raises the prospect that we might have to consider many virtues before deciding how to act. The upshot is that, on Russell's account, without knowing what all of the virtues are, virtue ethics will not be able to "say what right action is action in accordance with, or what it would be to be a virtuous person" (Russell 2009, 145). In addition, according to Russell (2009, 172), human psychology is finite, and thus, precludes the possibility of infinitely many virtues. There are only so many virtues that we are capable of having and acting on in the first place. But how can we know what the virtues are, much less be able to name them on a list? Russell (2009, 149) does not think that Aristotle provides much help with this, and looks to Plato, the Stoics, and Aquinas, who follows the Stoics, in adopting four cardinal or primary virtues, namely, justice, temperance, wisdom, and courage, and arguing that other virtues are related to these four by way of subordination (Russell 2009, 148–150). Russell's detailed account cannot be fully reviewed here, but a key feature is his claim that subordinate virtues are related to primary ones by shared general reasons, and not by the contexts in which they are exercised. For example, the same kinds of reasons that lead us to perform generous actions in ordinary situations would also apply to magnanimity – the virtue of giving lavishly in certain contexts. To illustrate, the same general kinds of reasons that I use when I give a gift to a friend – wanting her to be happy or better off in some way – also apply to giving on a grander scale, as when the Gates Foundation makes grants for education or an end to world poverty.

Elsewhere I argue against this approach to the enumeration problem (see Snow 2019). Russell is led to this position by his account of virtue ethical right action. He argues that virtue ethical right action must be virtuous *overall*; that is, it must take into account all of our serious practical concerns. How extensive must the consideration of all serious practical concerns be in order to generate the assessment that an action is, on virtue ethical grounds, the right one to perform in a given situation? In particular, must the consideration of all serious practical concerns in any given situation include knowledge of and attention to any and all of the virtues that might appear on a finite list of the virtues? Cases could readily arise in which some virtues have no bearing on whether a specific action would be virtue ethically right in a given circumstance, such that reference to those virtues would not arise in a consideration of all serious practical concerns arising in the situation. A parent deliberating about the distribution of limited resources between two equally deserving children might need to balance justice and generosity, for example, but need she be aware that temperance, magnificence, and ready wit are virtues on Aristotle's list? Would courage be implicated in her decision? Knowledge of and attention to a range of virtues would not be necessary to perform an action that would be deemed virtue ethically right overall. In other words, for any number of plausible cases, neither the existence of a finite list of virtues, nor the knowledge of all of the virtues on the list, is necessary to satisfy Russell's criterion for virtue ethical right action.

Russell's argument does not take sufficiently into account the fact that virtues typically pertain to spheres of life (see Nussbaum 1988). Russell (2014, 217, n. 26) seems to recognize this point, but is skeptical of its force: "It is likely that Aristotle thought the virtues should cover all of the 'key areas' of life (e.g., one's finances, emotions like fear and confidence, etc.), but it is far from obvious either that Aristotle's catalog does cover all such areas or that he thought it did. It is even less obvious how to identify such 'key areas,' how to individuate them, and how to know when they have all been identified." I think that Aristotle's virtues give us more guidance about identifying key areas of life than Russell allows, and that, with sufficient reflection, we can amplify Aristotle's account and identify key areas and the virtues that pertain to them. In this spirit, Kamtekar (2004, 481) remarks:

It seems open, then, to an Aristotelian to admit as new domains for practical attention those features of situations that social psychology identifies as particularly consequential for action: in the domain of group effects, there might be a virtue of taking appropriate account of the judgments of others; in the domain of time, a virtue of appropriate punctuality, and so on.

Cultural variations in virtues also present problems for Russell's approach. For example, the Korean virtue of *nunchi* is something like social intelligence, is integral to Korean society and its emphasis on interpersonal harmony, and cannot be easily correlated with the virtues on traditional Western lists (see Robertson 2019). Yet I would not want to deny its importance or its status as a virtue in Korean society; moreover, *nunchi* could well be a virtue that Westerners would do well to seek to understand and cultivate.

If these considerations are on the right track, then it seems we should not look to shared reasons for ways of unifying finite sets of virtues or relating them to one another, but, instead, to different spheres of life and cultural influences, with an eye to seeing how many virtues have been or could be developed in those contexts. The list of virtues would then be neither finite nor infinite, but, instead, indefinite, and would be grounded in the limits of shared human nature, thus avoiding the specter of cultural relativism. It would also be true that Russell's criterion of virtue ethical right action would need to be revised to provide a more nuanced account of the extent of serious practical considerations – including virtues – that should be considered in the performance of virtue ethical right action. Going back to Aunt Edna's hat, there has to be a time when reflection on serious practical concerns ends if we want to give her an answer when she asks us. Sometimes this practical reflection needs to take place on the spot, within definite time constraints. We should be able to give an answer that is virtue ethically right – perhaps by going back to a version of Hursthouse's criterion and asking what a virtuous person would characteristically do in the situation. The virtuous person, it seems to me, would try to be gentle as well as honest, and this might require some tactful evasiveness, especially if others are present. Of course, we have already seen the limits of Hursthouse's criterion, but at least it provides some guidance for how to think about virtuous action that might be helpful on the spot. The point is that a criterion of virtue ethical right action should not be so immersed in theory that it becomes impotent in practice. This takes us back to an insight of Aristotle's: ethics is an inexact science (*Nicomachean Ethics* 1094b14). It is inexact precisely because it is so rooted in the practicalities of living.

This conclusion, however, leaves us hanging. If we cannot specify a finite list of virtues, how can we know what kinds of persons to be? Virtue ethics is centrally concerned with character and its role in good lives. Can we be said to have good character if we are just but not brave, kind but not honest? The question, "What kind of people are good people?," is one with which philosophers have struggled, ever since ancient philosophers gave the answer: "Good people are those who possess all of the virtues, and one cannot have any of the virtues unless one has them all." This has been called the 'unity of virtues' thesis, and we need to examine versions of it to get more insight into what a good person looks like from a virtue ethical perspective. In addition, we need to know more about how good people develop. Our next topics, then, will be the unity of virtues and virtue development.

1.6 What Is a Good Person?

1.6.1 The Unity of Virtues

The unity of virtues thesis is also called the 'reciprocity of virtues' thesis. Aristotle maintains that one cannot have any virtue unless one has them all (see Aristotle *Nicomachean Ethics* VI 13.1144b30–1145a a2; Russell 2014, 213). On Aristotle's view, practical wisdom is necessary for every virtue, and every virtue is connected to every other through practical wisdom. Thus, one cannot have any virtue without possessing all of the others.

This thesis is highly counterintuitive. Suppose that Alex is kind but not brave. According to the strong thesis, we would have to deny that Alex is truly kind because he lacks bravery. This seems wrong. Many philosophers, neo-Aristotelian virtue ethicists as well as others, have struggled to make the unity thesis more palatable or to find more appealing versions or interpretations (e.g., Watson 1984; Flanagan 1991, 261ff; Lemos 1994; Badhwar 1996; Hursthouse 1999, 153–157; Swanton 2003; Wolf 2007; Russell 2009, chapter 11; and Russell 2014, 213–217). To the best of my knowledge, the only contemporary philosopher who holds the thesis in its strong form is John McDowell (1979). Similar in some respects to Badhwar (1996) and Watson (1984), Hursthouse (1999, 156) claims that, "anyone who possesses one virtue will have all the others to some degree, albeit, in some cases, a pretty limited one." This, too, seems unlikely. If I have known Alex for years and he has been consistently kind but has never once shown an ounce of courage, why would we want to insist that he is brave just because we recognize that he possesses kindness?

The unity thesis has traditionally been understood as a claim about the attribution of virtues to individuals. Russell (2014, 215–216; 2009, chapter 11) argues for a new twist: instead of regarding it as an attributive thesis, we should interpret it as a claim about the "natural makeup of the virtues" (2009, 362) and an ideal to which we should aspire. (He [2014, 215] notes that Aristotle does not advance the unity thesis as aspirational.) According to Russell (2009, 371–372), the natural makeup of the virtues is such that, unified by *phronēsis*, they ideally develop together in a balanced and integrated way. Interpreted as an aspirational ideal, we should expect improvement in one virtue to contribute to, and even require, improvement in others as virtuous sensitivities develop and mature (Russell 2014, 216). Thus, Russell suggests that we take a broadly developmental perspective on how virtues can be unified within a person's character. Let us examine various approaches to virtue development, which will eventually bring us back to a version of how virtues are unified within character.

1.6.2 Virtue Development

Aristotle's remarks about virtue acquisition are notoriously scant, and consist mainly of comments made in Book II of the *Nicomachean Ethics*. With the exception of some important papers specifically on Aristotle's views of moral development (e.g., Burnyeat 1980, Vasilou 1996, and Curzer 2002), the question of how virtue is acquired has not received significant attention from virtue ethicists until quite recently. A breakthrough was the publication of Julia Annas' important book, *Intelligent Virtue* (2011). In this book, Annas takes her cue from ancient philosophers who believe that the acquisition of virtue is like the acquisition of a practical skill. Annas (2011) argues that virtues, like practical skills, should be deliberately cultivated.[13] Two motivational characteristics of learners are central to her account: the need to learn and the drive to aspire (Annas 2011, 16ff). Cognitive

---

[13] For more on Annas (2011), see Snow (2015).

characteristics, too, are important for learners. The learner must seek to go beyond mere imitation of a teacher or role model, to develop her own style of being virtuous in accordance with her own personality and circumstances, and to become flexible and intelligent in her virtuous actions and responses (Annas 2011, 17). Annas (2011, 10–20) also imposes the 'articulacy requirement': both teachers and learners must be able to offer explanatory reasons for how and why they act virtuously.

Russell (2015) also argues that Aristotle's view of virtue acquisition is best understood on a model of skill development.[14] He identifies the three main points of Aristotle's account of moral development:

- Moral development consists of acquiring certain long-term attributes (*hexeis*) called virtues.
- The virtues are acquired through practice and training that must ultimately be focused and directed. In other words, the virtues are like skills in how we go about acquiring them.
- The virtues combine the pursuit of certain kinds of goals with practical reasoning that is effective in making and executing plans for realizing those goals. In other words, the virtues are also like skills in their cognitive structure (Russell 2015, 30).

Russell maintains that virtues, and the ways in which we acquire them, are mundane – part and parcel of everyday life. That is, the virtues are rational excellences, which, like other human excellences, are ways of being good at something within the human sphere of life (Russell 2015, 22). Aristotle's approach to virtue development is, to use a term from psychology, 'path-dependent,' in the sense that it starts from general knowledge of what is known about how people develop and extends it to the improvement of character (Russell 2015, 19). Russell (2015, 19–20) contrasts this approach with the 'path-independent' method taken by Lawrence Kohlberg, who argued that moral improvement is a matter of moving through stages that are predetermined in accordance with formal, universal moral principles.

Other recent forays into virtue development include Kristjánsson (2015) and Snow (2018c). Kristjánsson (2015) argues for a theory of Aristotelian character development that can be integrated into schools. Snow (2018c) contends that mature individuals can progress from 'ordinary' to Aristotelian virtue through the pursuit of valued goals. This progression depends upon the deepening recognition of the different kinds of value – instrumental, constitutive, and intrinsic – that virtue can have, in conjunction with the development of phronetic

---

[14] Another interesting approach is taken by Athanassoulis (2018).

capacities. Wright, Warren, and Snow (in press) offer even more recent work on the development and integration of virtues. There, they advance the 'integration thesis' as an alternative to the 'unity' or 'reciprocity' thesis. According to the integration thesis, which is a practical claim about virtue development, virtues develop together in response to the circumstances of daily life. Consider, for example, a common scenario: a child sees and responds to another child's bullying of a playmate. She could respond in any number of ways, but suppose that she defends the bullied child and seeks to convince the bully that what he or she is doing in unfair and unkind. The first child's responses to external factors are important mechanisms of virtue development because they are among her initial forays into the exercise of virtue. Initially, the child's responses to the situations she encounters are quite primitive (ethically speaking), since she is, in large part, simply following her own feelings or the guidance of others. These initial responses cannot be called 'virtuous' because her practical wisdom has yet to develop. As children's reason develops, they become more able to act virtuously of their own accord and use practical reason in choosing when and how to act virtuously. At some point in development, the capacity for reason should enable them to take a reflective stance on their behavior, and come to endorse it. Eventually, we hope, children come to see the value in generous or kind behavior, and it becomes ingrained as part of their emerging characters.

At this point in the section, we have a fairly comprehensive overview of recent work in neo-Aristotelian virtue ethics. Starting from a brief overview of Aristotle's ethics, we've investigated the reasons for turning to virtue ethics as an alternative to deontology and utilitarianism, have examined advances made in the early stages of the turn, then plunged into efforts by Hursthouse and Russell to develop a form of virtue ethics that seeks to address central issues of virtue ethical right action and the question of whether there is, or needs to be, a finite list of the virtues. We concluded this theoretical overview with the questions of what the character of a virtuous person looks like, and how virtues are developed.

This is not the end of the story, however, for one further question remains to be addressed, namely, "How is the project of neo-Aristotelian virtue ethics justified?" This is related to a critique mentioned earlier: that of moral relativism. Neither Aristotle nor neo-Aristotelians believe that moral standards are culturally or societally relative. Instead, they seek to ground claims about virtue in human nature. To this project we now turn.

1.7 Ethical Naturalism

Aristotle's ethics is naturalistic; that is, it does not look to nonnatural factors, such as Plato's Form of the Good, or divine commands, which go beyond the realm of nature or humanity, to justify ethics. [15] Instead, Aristotle believes that ethics is grounded in human nature. In other words, being virtuous – developing and practicing the virtues as rational excellences – is how we fulfill our human natures. If this is true, then it is not the case that virtues are culturally relative – they are grounded in our natures as human beings. This is the insight that Nussbaum (1988) draws upon in her paper – humans, no matter their society or culture, share commonalities. Among other things, we all need to eat, drink, reproduce, and form familial and social bonds. We make choices within these and other spheres of life. The virtues should, ideally, regulate our choices.

Contemporary neo-Aristotelians expand on the notion of human nature that grounds our virtuous activity.[16] Here I review central features of the approach taken by Rosalind Hursthouse, Philippa Foot, and Michael Thompson, which I take to be the dominant conception of neo-Aristotelian ethical naturalism, with special focus on the work of Foot and Thompson.

The central idea of this approach is that evaluations of the moral goodness and badness of humans have the same conceptual structure as evaluations of the goodness and badness of plants and animals. These judgments provide standards by means of which we can identify individuals that are good of their kind and those that are defective. Since it is the nature of wolves to hunt together in packs and the nature of dancing bees to lead other bees to sources of nectar, we can say that a free-riding wolf, one who does not participate in the hunt but partakes of the spoils, and a dancing bee who finds nectar but does not alert other bees to its whereabouts, are defective. They are just as defective in these social aspects as are members of species who suffer from individual defects, for example, who lack sight, hearing, or the power of movement (see Foot 2002, 200). Moral evaluations, Foot (2002, 200) claims, are like the evaluations of natural goodness and defect in plants and animals. That said, she acknowledges the extent to which human communication and reason complicate these evaluations, not least by creating a diversity of goods exceeding those available to plants and other animals in extent and complexity.

Both Foot and Hursthouse expand on this basic picture and draw on an important paper by Michael Thompson, "The Representation of Life," which develops a conceptual structure for naturalistic evaluations of plants, animals, and humans (see Hursthouse 1999 and 2004; Foot 2001;; Thompson 1995). Thompson amplifies this structure in his later work (see Thompson 2003, 2004, 2008, and 2013). A starting point for understanding his view is his development of the abstract concept of a 'natural kind' into the notion of

---

[15] This section draws on Snow (2018b and 2019).

[16] Notable contributors are McDowell (1998), MacIntyre (1999), Hursthouse (1999, 2004), Foot (2001), and Thompson (1995, 2003, 2004, 2008, 2013).

a life-form. A life-form is the idea of a living kind or species (Thompson 1995, 266). Knowledge of life-forms enables us to make life-form attributions, the general form of which is: "*X is a bearer of life form S*, or *X is a member of species S* ..., " and natural historical judgments (Thompson 2004, 58, italics his; see also 2004, 49 and 1995, 280ff). Natural historical judgments describe life-forms, and take the form: "'The *S* is (or has, or does) *F*,'" as in "'The domestic cat has four legs, two eyes, two ears, and guts in its belly'" (see Thompson 1995, 281). These are statements of facts about species on which the good of individual species members depends (see Thompson 1995, 281). If Tibbles the cat has only three legs, but not four, he is lacking in a feature on which his good as a member of the feline species depends (see Thompson 2008, 65). Natural historical judgments are normative in allowing for inferences of the type: 'The S is F,' 'this S is not F,' therefore, 'this S is defective in not being an F' (see Thompson 1995, 295). Through this type of inference, we arrive at judgments of the natural goodness or defectiveness of individual members of species. To illustrate, if we know that Tibbles is a cat (life-form attribution), that cats have four legs (natural historical judgment), and that Tibbles has only three legs, we can say that Tibbles is defective because he does not have four legs.

This scheme applies to Foot's work because operations of the will or practical reason in humans are species-dependent and thus, can be judged as good or bad according to a natural standard. Our species is the kind of life-form whose natural history shows us to be capable of acting well, for reasons that we see as good (see Thompson 2004, 59ff and 1995, 250–251). Thus, when we fail to see reasons as good and do not act upon them, or see them as good yet fail to act, we are displaying defects, and if someone fails chronically in these ways, she can be judged a defective member of the human species. These judgments have the same conceptual structure and follow the same logic as attributions of goodness and defect to other species. To illustrate, if I see someone being bullied but do not see that as a reason to act in their defense, or if I see her being bullied as a good reason to act but am afraid to do so, those are defects on my part. If I chronically fail to see bullying as a reason to act in defense of another, or see it as a good reason to act but am afraid to do so, I can be called defective as a human being. My defect is in my will to act, and is on a par with defective hearing or sight.

The account of ethical naturalism as sketched here has come in for criticism, even within the camp of ethical naturalists (see, for example, Toner 2008). Scientifically minded critics have taken issue with it.[17] Moosavi (2018, 296), for

---

[17] Such critics include FitzPatrick (2000), Copp and Sobel (2004, 532–543), Woodcock (2006), Andreou (2006), Millgram (2009), Lewens (2010, 2012), Odenbaugh (2017), and Moosavi (2018). For defenses see, for example, Hursthouse (2012) and Lott (2012).

example, claims that ethical naturalism "relies on commonsense descriptions of living things rather than state-of-the-art science." She notes that this is a problem of "naturalistic credentials"; ethical naturalism does not comport well with nature as scientists understand it (see Moosavi 2018, 282–279). Millgram (2009, 559) writes in the same vein when he calls what Thompson is doing the "method of the nature documentary." The question of how well ethical naturalism does, or should, comport with contemporary science is beyond the scope of this section, but is indicative of some of the lively debates to which virtue ethics gives rise.

1.8 Conclusion

I have sought to motivate this section by approaching a number of issues of central importance for contemporary neo-Aristotelian virtue ethics. After an initial overview of Aristotle's theory, we delved into the question of why the turn to virtue ethics was made. This led us into sophisticated attempts to expound virtue ethics as a well-developed theoretical alternative to deontology and consequentialism. Questions of action guidance and thus, of virtue ethical right action are central to that project. Crucial to the articulation of a virtue ethical criterion of right action are the questions of what the virtues are, what the character of the good person is like, that is, what virtues should she have, and how those virtues develop. Finally, we looked at ethical naturalism, which tries to ground virtues as universal moral standards that are not culturally or societally relative. Of necessity, we had to omit certain topics, such as eudaimonism. We also had to omit Aristotle's views on emotions, friendship, and political community.[18] Yet attention to these topics, too, adds to ongoing work in neo-Aristotelian virtue ethics. We turn now to Section 2, which discusses virtue ethical alternatives to neo-Aristotelianism.

2 Alternatives to Neo-Aristotelian Virtue Ethics

Many philosophers are sympathetic to virtue ethics, but have found neo-Aristotelian approaches unsatisfying, and so have stepped outside the Aristotelian tradition in their thinking about virtue. In the last twenty years or so, many creative alternative accounts have been advanced. For example, Thomas Hurka puts forward his recursive account in *Virtue, Vice, and Value* (2001). Robert Merrihew Adams presents Platonist theories in his books *Finite and Infinite Goods: A Framework for Ethics* (1999) and *A Theory of Virtue: Excellence in Being for the Good* (2006). Sophie-Grace Chappell develops

---

[18] See, for example, Kristjánsson (2018a) and Riesbeck (2016).

a Platonist account that is inspired by the philosopher Iris Murdoch in *Knowing What To Do: Imagination, Virtue, and Platonism in Ethics* (2017). Feminist virtue ethics was developed by Lisa Tessman in *Burdened Virtues: Virtue Ethics for Liberatory Struggles* (2005), and has been critiqued by fellow feminists Macalester Bell (2006), Cheshire Calhoun (2008), Marilyn Friedman (2009), and Robin Dillon (2018). Very recently, Nicholas Bommarito's book *Inner Virtue* (2018) was published. Another recent book is Matt Stichter's *The Skillfulness of Virtue: Improving Our Moral and Epistemic Lives* (2018), in which Stichter argues that virtue is a kind of skill. Even more recently, Irene McMullin presents an account of virtue and flourishing that is informed by existential phenomenology in her book, *Existential Flourishing: A Phenomenology of the Virtues* (2019). An informed discussion of all of this work on virtue would overwhelm readers. For this reason, I have focused on what I regard as the main contributions to alternatives to neo-Aristotelian virtue ethics, as found in work by Christine Swanton, Michael Slote, Linda Zagzebski, and Michael S. Brady. To this we now turn.

2.1 Christine Swanton (2003): Non-Eudaimonistic Pluralism

In *Virtue Ethics: A Pluralistic View* (2003), Christine Swanton offers an alternative that she has called 'non-eudaimonistic pluralism.'[19] She writes: "A *virtue* is a good quality of character, more specifically a disposition to respond to, or acknowledge, items within its field or fields in an excellent or good enough way" (Swanton 2003, 19; emphasis hers). As Glen Pettigrove (2018, 367) helpfully summarizes in his discussion of Swanton, to understand a virtue we need to understand four components: (1) its field; (2) its mode of responsiveness; (3) its basis of moral acknowledgment; and (4) its target.[20]

The field of a virtue is the area of life with which it is concerned. Temperance, for example, regulates bodily pleasures and objects of desire; courage, by contrast, is concerned with dangerous situations. A virtue's mode of responsiveness concerns how virtues shape our responses to items in their fields. For example, we might respect an individual in virtue of her status, promote the good of a friend or stranger, honor someone's achievement, appreciate or value a work of art, express creativity, and so on. Items in the field of a virtue make demands on us in virtue of certain

---

[19] In personal conversation some years ago, Swanton described the view she develops in Swanton (2003) as 'non-eudaimonistic pluralism.' I use it instead of the term used by Pettigrove (2018, 359), 'target-centered,' and in Hursthouse and Pettigrove (2018), because I believe it more aptly captures essential features of her work. Some of her more recent work on virtue ethics can be found in Swanton (2015) and (2018).

[20] See also Swanton (2003), 20–24, and Hursthouse and Pettigrove (2018).

kinds of features that they possess. These features are the bases of moral acknowledgment or responsiveness. For example, love responds to relational bonds; respect, to status; and generosity, to benefits. As Pettigrove (2018, 367) notes, Swanton's view is pluralist both about the bases of acknowledgment of the virtues and about the modes of virtuous responding. Finally, the target of a virtue is that at which it is aimed, and it will vary from virtue to virtue.

Given this scheme, Swanton (2003, 3) is able to introduce and develop what she calls the profile of a virtue, which is: "that constellation of modes of moral responsiveness or acknowledgement which comprise the virtuous disposition." Virtues, she thinks, typically have a complex profile insofar as they require an agent to respond to items in their fields through multiple modes. These modes express fine inner states of the agent.

Far more could be said about Swanton's view, but I wish to note only three further points. The first is that Swanton regards virtue as a threshold concept. This implies that the requirements for virtue are not set by a single standard, for example, the well-functioning member of the human species, as is found in neo-Aristotelian ethical naturalism, but, instead, "the standards are to some extent relative to the individual's own capacities (understood in a dynamic sense)" (Swanton 2003, 3). The second is that she argues extensively against the view that what makes a trait a virtue is that it partly constitutes and contributes to the flourishing or *eudaimonia* of its possessor. What makes a trait a virtue, she contends, is that "it is a disposition to respond in an excellent (or good enough) way" through the various modes of responding to items in the fields of the virtue (Swanton 2003, 93). She argues for what she calls the 'Constraint on Virtue': "A correct conception of the virtues must be at least partly shaped by a correct conception of healthy growth and development which in part constitute our flourishing" (Swanton 2003, 60). The Constraint on Virtue, she believes, does not entail eudaimonism. Finally, her account of virtue ethical right action is somewhat similar to Russell (2009)'s in that it introduces the notion that virtue ethical right action must be overall virtuous in any given situation. For Swanton (2003), this is because of the possibility of multiple types of pluralism: two virtues could respond to different bases within their fields, the fields of virtues might overlap, and it might not be possible to perform acts exemplifying the two virtues in any given situation. For Swanton (2003, 239–240), an act is right if and only if it is overall virtuous, and an act overall virtuous if and only if it is "the, or a, best action possible in the circumstances." An act is wrong if and only if it is overall vicious, and in between there are a range of actions that are good enough.[21]

---

[21] See Swanton (2003, 240), and Pettigrove's discussion of these points (2018, 368–369).

Swanton's rather complex alternative to neo-Aristotelian virtue ethics was not the first on the philosophical scene. Two other philosophers, Michael Slote and Linda Zagzebski, developed versions of a view called agent-basing in the mid-to-late 1990s, then went on to modify their approaches and provide interestingly different accounts of virtue in later work. Let us consider Slote first, then turn to Zagzebski.

2.2 Michael Slote: From Agent-Basing to Sentimentalism

Slote (1992, 1997, 2001) begins his work on virtue ethics with what has been called 'agent-based' virtue ethics, then departs from that perspective in interesting ways in Slote (2010, 2018), there championing moral sentimentalism.

Typically, approaches to virtue ethics are agent-focused in that they are interested in agents and their characteristics. However, agent-basing "treats the moral status of acts as derivative from independent and fundamental aretaic (as opposed to deontic) characterizations of motives, character traits or individuals."[22] Aretaic motives are those expressive of a concern for virtue, whereas deontic motives express a concern for duty, moral principles, or rule-following. Thus, a concern with being kind or courageous would count as an aretaic motive, whereas a concern with doing one's duty for duty's sake would be deontic. What matters for Slote are the actual motives and dispositions of agents at the time of acting; in other words, the goodness of an action is derived from the agent's motives when she performs the action.[23] Slote (2001) applies his agent-based approach extensively, using it to explain such topics as practical rationality, the human good, social justice, institutions, the state, and laws.

In Slote (2001, esp. chapter 3), he uses an ethics of care to justify and motivate central aspects of this discussion. In later work, he shifts to a sentimentalist approach in which empathy is the central concept.[24] He writes: "the virtue ethical sentimentalist holds, very roughly, that normative distinctions and motivations derive from emotion or sentiment rather than (practical) reason" (Slote 2018, 344). His later approach invokes the sentimentalist tradition of Francis Hutcheson and David Hume (he notes that Hutcheson was influenced by the Judeo-Christian tradition).[25] Slote (2018, 354) considers his approach to "be a form both of sentimentalist virtue ethics and of care ethics." However, he maintains that his sentimentalism differs in key respects from the care ethics advocated by the feminists and care theorists Nel Noddings and

---

[22] See Slote (2001, 5) and (1997, 206); quoted at Pettigrove (2018), 360); see also Slote (1992, 83–84).

[23] See also Hursthouse and Pettigrove (2018).   [24] See Slote (2010) and (2018).

[25] Slote (2018, 344–345) also discusses Buddhist and Confucian influences as part of the historical background of contemporary virtue ethical sentimentalism.

Virginia Held, most notably by being focused on the qualities or virtues of persons and not on caring relationships (Slote 2018, 354–355).

As we saw in our discussion of neo-Aristotelian theories, meta-ethical positions are often employed to support moral evaluations, that is, judgments of goodness and badness. Neo-Aristotelians such as Hursthouse, Foot, and Thompson have developed a version of ethical naturalism as a meta-ethical approach. Slote (2010) advances a sentimentalist meta-ethics to support sentimentalist virtue ethics and normative ethics more generally. His criterion of right action is that "an action is morally acceptable or all right if and only if it doesn't manifest or reflect a lack of empathic caringness on the part of the agent" (2018, 355). Empathy in these cases, he notes, is first order, but moral concepts involve second-order empathy. When we are empathically warmed by observing empathic first-order relations or empathically chilled by their absence, we manifest moral approval or disapproval. In other words, we know that something is right or wrong by the reactions of empathic warming (approval) or chilling (disapproval) that it elicits from us.

To conclude, Slote's later work is as least as expansive in its purview as his earlier work, if not more so, offering a sentimentalist perspective on a wide range of normative and meta-ethical issues, including objectivity, rationality, moral judgments, autonomy, respect, education, patriarchy, paternalism, autonomy, distributive justice, and international and global justice.

2.3 Linda Zagzebski: From Agent-Basing to Exemplar Theory

As with Slote, Linda Zagzebski begins her work on virtue with an account of agent-basing, then moves into different terrain. In her seminal early work, *Virtues of the Mind: An Inquiry into the Nature of Virtue and the Ethical Foundations of Knowledge* (1996), she offers a version of agent-based virtue ethics that she calls 'motivation-based.' The concept of a motivation is fundamental, and the concept of a virtue is defined in terms of a good motivation. The concept of a right act is then defined in terms of a virtue. A motive is a feeling or emotion that initiates and directs action toward an end (Zagzebski 1996, 131). Virtue is "a deep and enduring acquired excellence of a person, involving a characteristic motivation to produce a certain desired end and reliable success in bringing about that end" (Zagzebski 1996, 137). She defines 'right act' by starting with the notion of a wrong act: a wrong act is something a virtuous person would not do in the circumstances; that is, it is not permissible for a virtuous person to perform a wrong act in the circumstances. A right act is permissible (that is, not wrong), so, "A right act is what a virtuous person might do in certain circumstances," where "might" stands in for "would" (Zagzebski 1996, 233).

In addition to being a landmark work in virtue ethics, Zagzebski (1996) is a major contribution to virtue epistemology. Virtue epistemology seeks to understand traditional problems in epistemology, or the theory of knowledge, such as the nature of knowledge, how we are justified in what we know, and how we can meet the challenge of skepticism, through a virtue-based framework. Zagzebski advances a responsibilist theory of intellectual virtues, according to which intellectual virtues, such as open-mindedness and curiosity, are types of traits. Other virtue epistemologists, such as Ernest Sosa and John Greco, are reliabilists.[26] For them, intellectual or epistemic virtues are kinds of capacities, such as perception, memory, and attention.

In later work, especially in her book, *Exemplarist Moral Theory* (2017), Zagzebski develops exemplarist moral theory.[27] She has a "theory of moral theories": moral theories, she argues, can be viewed analogously to maps (2010, 39–47; 2017, 5–9). Both are meant to help us find our way around a particular terrain, and both can be more or less detailed and emphasize different features of what they are maps or theories of. Moral theories simplify, systematize, and justify moral beliefs and practices, using a variety of moral concepts. Different theories emphasize different moral concepts, working primarily with three main ones: the right, the good, and virtue.

We saw how this works in Section 1, in Hursthouse (1999)'s approach to developing virtue ethics as a theoretical alternative to deontology and utilitarianism. Zagzebski takes note of this basic framework: deontological theories prioritize the right, giving both the good and virtue subsidiary roles, whereas consequentialist theories accord the good pride of place, defining right actions and virtuous traits as those that bring about the good. Virtue ethics take virtue to be the primary concept in terms of which goodness (flourishing) is obtained, and in terms of which right action might be defined. Each of these theory types is foundationalist in structure, identifying one fundamental concept – the right, the good, and virtue, respectively – as the basis in terms of which the others are defined. Exemplar theory follows suit in being foundationalist, but differs in that the foundation is not a concept, but, instead, exemplars of moral goodness. We identify figures such as Confucius, Jesus Christ, and others as exemplars of moral goodness through our feelings of admiration for them (Zagzebski 2017, 10). Thus, unlike other types of moral theory, Zagzebski's proceeds by identifying morally exemplary individuals as foundational, and defining moral terms, such as 'right act,' as what they would do, and moral properties, such as

---

[26] See Sosa (2007, 2009) and Greco (2010).　　[27] See also Zagzebski (2010).

'virtues,' as their admirable traits (Zagzebski 2017, 21–22). Thus, exemplars provide a "hook" to link Zagzebski's theory with moral practices, as well as with moral education and empirical study (Zagzebski 2017, 7–8). Moreover, though we can disagree about which individuals we find admirable, we can, as a community, agree about many of them, and it only takes a few exemplars, she thinks, to get her theory off the ground (Zagzebski 2017, 10).

Zagzebski draws on the philosophy of language in the construction of her account of virtue. Thus, to understand the first move in the construction of exemplar theory, we need to understand the difference between the descriptive theory of reference and the version of the theory of direct reference that Zagzebski adopts.[28] According to the descriptive theory, we know the meaning of a term when we grasp the description of it that is given in a dictionary, and a user of the term designates whatever object matches that description. This theory works well for artifacts such as 'hammer,' 'cup,' and so on, but not for proper names or natural kind terms, such as 'water' or 'gold.' As Zagzebski (2017, 11) writes: "The meaning of 'water' cannot be 'colorless, odorless liquid in the lakes and streams and falling from the sky,' or any other description that we use in ordinary discourse to pick out water." This is because we can imagine something of the same description that is not in fact water. In other words, we might sometimes mistake a colorless, odorless liquid for water, but that does not prevent us from correctly identifying water on many other occasions. What makes water what it is is that it is H_2O. But the meaning of water cannot be H_2O, since people knew what water was long before the molecular structure of water was identified, and the meaning of 'water' did not change with that discovery. When its molecular structure was discovered, we found out "the nature of something that people had been talking about all along" (Zagzebski 2017, 11).

Zagzebski uses these ideas to generate her theory of moral exemplars. We identify moral exemplars through our feeling of admiration, which enables us to pick out the superficial features of morally exemplary individuals – for example, we might admire Confucius for his wisdom, or Jesus Christ for his love and compassion. We do not need to know the descriptive meanings of 'wisdom,' 'love,' or 'compassion' to make these identifications. However, admiration does not give us access to the deep psychological features of exemplars. Zagzebski (2017, 20) believes that further study of exemplars can yield insights into their moral psychologies. Narratives, that is, stories about exemplars, as well as scientific study, contribute to this undertaking.

The feeling of admiration allows us not only to identify exemplars, but also motivates us to be like them – it makes us want to imitate the exemplar

---

[28] See Zagzebski (2017, 10–14).

(Zagzebski 2017, 20). There are many complexities involved with this, which Zagzebski addresses throughout the course of her book. What happens if our admiration misses the mark, if we admire someone who is not worthy of being an exemplar? Zagzebski thinks that our emotional reactions can be judged by our communities, and that it is not possible for communities to radically disagree about who is an exemplar (Zagzebski 2017, 17). This is because humans have the same nature, the same emotional dispositions, psychological tendencies, and so on. If one community consistently admired people who were nasty and brutish, Zagzebski thinks it would be doubtful that they would be in the same species as us.

My view is that the question of radical disagreement about exemplars is not so easily set aside. We live in an age of widespread political polarization, in which many countries are seeing the rise of extreme political views. Today not only isolated individuals, but entire communities, seem to admire and seek to emulate such figures as Adolf Hitler, Viktor Orbán, Marine Le Pen, Narendra Modi, Jair Bolsonaro, and other far-right political types. Admirers of such people have either not been given or have not been receptive to guidance about the inappropriateness of taking these individuals to be exemplary. This issue is a serious one: some people admire these individuals because they advocate immoral views, such as racism and anti-Semitism, yet we do not think these admirers are of a different species from the rest of us.

This issue is similar to, yet distinct from, another problem that exemplarist moral theory needs to address, namely, that in which someone admires a person for a genuinely praiseworthy trait or skill, yet the person who is admired also has negative traits. Young people, for example, often admire athletes or musicians for their prowess in sports or music, yet their heroes might also be guilty of substance abuse or domestic violence. These aspects of exemplar theory are ripe for further examination.

A further question about exemplarism is this. Is humility a necessary virtue of exemplars? Studies of Canadians who have received awards for being brave and caring suggest that the recipients possess humility – they are not arrogant or self-congratulatory (see Walker and Frimer 2007). Similarly, Holocaust res-cuers often downplay their heroism, suggesting that they were only doing their duty, or that anyone would have done the same (see Oliner and Oliner 1988). This is in tune with the idea that it would detract from the overall goodness of an exemplar if he or she were "puffed up" and arrogant about her moral goodness. One cannot imagine Jesus Christ boasting about the miracles he performed, or Gandhi bragging about his nonviolent efforts to free India from British rule. These reflections suggest the beginnings of an argument that humility is an essential aspect of moral exemplars.

2.4 Brady (2018): Suffering and Virtue

In an innovative recent contribution to the literature on virtue, *Suffering and Virtue* (2018), Michael S. Brady argues that suffering is essential for the goods and virtues necessary for happiness and flourishing. He develops a desire view of suffering, according to which "suffering is negative affect that we *mind*, where minding is cashed out in terms of an *occurrent desire* that the negative affect not be occurring" (Brady 2018, 5; emphasis his). Suffering thus conceived, he argues, is essential for virtue. It is essential for virtue in three ways: by having constitutive, developmental, and communicative value.

Dispositions to suffer have constitutive value for virtue by actually being, under certain conditions, virtuous motives of certain pain and emotional systems. The epistemic and motivational roles that suffering plays within the proper operation of these systems allow us to respond well to a range of negative objects and events. We need to be able to perceive these objects and events, recognize their importance, and be motivated to respond appropriately (Brady 2018, 3). Pain and remorse, for example, can be what Brady calls 'faculty' virtues, which, like sight, operate within the contexts of larger systems, enabling us, in appropriate circumstances, to identify and be motivated to achieve certain goods that are essential to flourishing. Provided that forms of physical and emotional suffering outperform other feasible alternatives in allowing us to attain these goods, they can be said to constitute virtuous motives. Brady (2018) develops detailed arguments for this position in chapter 4 of his book, but his point is succinctly stated as follows: "I will ... defend the following radical claim: that physical and emotional suffering itself can *be* virtuous, since it plays vital epistemic and motivational roles in bringing about the good at which our physical and motivational systems aim" (Brady 2018, 84; emphasis his). For example, the disposition to suffer pain is essential for the proper functioning of physical systems that regulate damage avoidance and repair; and remorse can be essential for an emotional system whose goods include reparation and atonement (Brady 2018, 61).

This interesting and controversial position on the constitutive value of suffering for virtue could be explicated in far more detail, but here I will mention only one objection and Brady's reply (see Brady 2018, 80–83). The objection is that we typically view suffering as intrinsically evil, and virtue as intrinsically good. But if so, it seems impossible to claim that suffering is an intrinsically good virtuous motive, even when carefully qualified by a range of conditions. Brady (2018) addresses this objection by invoking a distinction between what I will call 'stand-alone' intrinsic goods and those that are intrinsically good in virtue of their relations to stand-alone intrinsic goods.[29] To illustrate, Brady (2018, 80–81) asks us to consider that remorse is intrinsically bad when considered by itself. However, when considered in relation to wrongdoing, it amounts to hating what is evil, and is an appropriate response considered as part of that intrinsically valuable relation. He writes: "The thought would be, then, that an intrinsically bad mental state – such as remorse – can be part of an intrinsically valuable relation when it is directed toward something else that is intrinsically bad – like wrongdoing" (Brady 2018, 81). In other words, "the negatively valenced attitudes can be part of positively valenced relations " (Brady 2018, 81).

In later chapters of the book, Brady (2018) develops the notion that suffering can be developmentally valuable insofar as it enables us to attain certain virtues which allow us to achieve goods necessary for flourishing. For example, suffering can help us to develop the virtue of strength of character as we struggle with adversity, and it can assist us in acquiring what he calls the 'virtues of vulnerability' – virtues such as adaptability, creativity, humility, and intimacy – which can be edifying in enabling us to cope with physical illness and incapacity and in confronting our own mortality. Suffering can also help us to attain moral virtues and the virtue of wisdom. Finally, suffering has communicative value inasmuch as it is essential for justice, loving relationships, and faith and trust. To make his case for this, Brady (2018, 9) draws initially on religious teachings, but also extends it to the secular, arguing that: "these forms of suffering will be a feature of properly functioning relationships and social groups in secular spheres."

As a contribution to philosophical thought on virtue, Brady's book is groundbreaking in at least two significant respects. First, it invites secular philosophers to think more deeply about the value of suffering in human life, and whether and how it can be a virtue that can help those who suffer to have some kind or degree of flourishing. In this respect, Brady (2018) could have importance for psychologists, such as Eranda Jayawickreme and Laura Blackie (2016), who investigate the possibility of strength through adversity.

Second, Brady's focus on suffering is suggestive inasmuch as it invites philosophers to investigate other negative life events through the lens of virtue ethics. It is widely recognized by educators, for example, that many students suffer from trauma. The causes of this trauma are varied: hunger, poverty, unstable home lives, substance abuse by parents or caretakers, even sexual

---

[29] To make this argument, Brady (2018) embraces Thomas Hurka's recursive account in *Virtue, Vice, and Value* (2001, 17), according to which hating what is evil is intrinsically good because it is a morally appropriate response to what is evil. Readers will recall that I mentioned Hurka's book at the beginning of this section.

and physical abuse. In other words, as individuals, some students have been traumatized. Others suffer from 'collective' forms of trauma, for example, by being members of populations that have been subjected to war and attempts at genocide, or who have historically suffered or presently endure discrimination. Jews, African-Americans, Latinx, indigenous populations, and LGBTQI populations of which they are members all have histories of discrimination and of ill-treatment by others.[30] Immigrants to the United States from certain countries, such as Central American and Muslim nations, also endure discrimination simply because of their group membership. These tragic situations not only undermine the capacities of students to learn, they also affect their abilities to develop virtue and character. To be maximally effective, our efforts to cultivate virtue in traumatized populations must engage in nuanced work in the area of moral repair, seeking to understand the effects that various forms of trauma can have on the psychological and emotional capacities needed for the acquisition of virtue.

This second point, of course, is not unrelated to the first. The "take-home" message is that Brady's work on suffering and virtue should inspire philosophers to engage in similarly deep and nuanced studies of various kinds of trauma, how they can undermine capacities for virtue development, how moral repair can take place, and what virtues might be available to members of different groups who have been traumatized. How can the growth of virtue take place in people who have been harmed in different ways? What would their virtue development look like, and what kinds of virtues would best contribute to the flourishing of those who have suffered?[31]

2.5 Conclusion

The aim of this section has been to give readers a sample of the depth and complexity of alternatives to neo-Aristotelian virtue ethics. We saw interesting theoretical advances in the work of all of the authors discussed here, but we also saw, to my mind, a groundbreaking development by Brady (2018) – a full-scale attempt to show how the negative life experience of suffering can either be a virtue or can contribute to virtue. As the foregoing discussion indicates, work in alternative approaches to neo-Aristotelian virtue ethics proceeds with at least as much vigor as work in the neo-Aristotelian tradition, if not more so. Yet virtue ethics, whether in the neo-Aristotelian tradition or outside of it, has been critiqued. In the next section, I consider and reply to two main objections.

---

[30] The acronym 'LGBTQI' stands for "lesbian, gay, bisexual, transgender, queer, and intersex."

[31] Some studies of this have already taken place with members of the military and veterans who suffer from post-traumatic stress disorder (PTSD). See, for example, the work of the philosopher Nancy Sherman, especially Sherman (2015).

3 Objections to Virtue Ethics

Virtue ethics has not been without its detractors. As we saw in Section 1, virtue ethics has been criticized for its alleged inability to provide a virtue ethical criterion of right action. The claim has also been made that virtue ethics is morally relativist. For more on the first topic, I refer interested readers to Johansson and Svensson (2018), for discussion of the second, to Stangl (2018). Here I discuss two other objections: what has been called the egoism or self-centeredness objection, and the situationist challenge to virtue ethics.

3.1 The Egoism or Self-Centeredness Objection

One important objection to virtue ethics, especially eudaimonistic versions in which flourishing predominates, is that it is egoistic or self-centered; that is, it takes the agent's concern for his own flourishing as paramount at the expense of morally legitimate concern for others.[32] Christopher Toner (2006, 595) lists a number of complaints, for example, from Thomas Nagel (1986, 195–197), that Aristotle's ethics fails to give due value to the claims of others; from H. A. Prichard (1995, 45–46), that Aristotle's ethics suggests that our only business in life is self-improvement; and from Immanuel Kant (1993) that making one happy is different from making one good, and that making one prudent is different from making one virtuous. In *Virtue, Vice, and Value*, Thomas Hurka (2001, 138) contends that "self-indulgence consists only in caring 'disproportionately' about one's virtue, or having it be 'more important' in one's motivation than a concern for other people." He claims (2001, 246): "it is again not virtuous – it is morally self-indulgent – to act primarily from concern for one's own virtue."

Scholars of Aristotle's work have discussed the objection specifically with respect to his eudaimonistic ethics, but more recently, Toner (2006, 2010) has cast a wider net, discussing contemporary virtue ethicists, including Hursthouse and Swanton, as well as Aristotle and Aquinas.[33] Toner (2006, 599–600) helpfully distinguishes two levels of motivation: what the philosopher Shelly Kagan (1998) calls 'factors' and 'foundations.' The basic distinction is that we can have reasons that motivate us at the level of acting (factors) and those that

---

[32] See, for example, Toner (2010, 275). Aretaic virtue ethics, such as developed by Slote (2001), could also be liable to the charge of self-centeredness, but here I focus on the discussion as applicable primarily to Aristotelian virtue ethics. Additionally, Toner (2006, 595–596) distinguishes egoism from self-centeredness, but I do not think anything hinges upon this distinction here. The key claim is that the virtuous person privileges herself at the expense of others, and does so for the sake of her own flourishing.

[33] Scholars who discuss egoism and self–other concern in Aristotle include Howard Curzer (2012), Dennis McKerlie (1998), Julia Annas (1993, 1992, 1988), Richard Kraut (1989), Terence Irwin (1988), and Marcia Homiak (1981).

motivate us at a deeper level (foundations). At the level of factors, eudaimonistic virtue ethics seems to avoid the charge of self-centeredness. Hursthouse (1999, 128–129), for example, notes that reasons such as 'You need it more than I do,' readily serve as virtuous reasons for acting.[34] Such reasons seem able adequately to account for the concerns of others, and do not privilege the self over others' claims in ways that fall foul of moral standards. But at the deeper level of foundations, the self-centeredness problem arises again. Hurka (2001, 246) puts the point as follows:

> A flourishing-based theory . . . says that a person has reason to act rightly only or ultimately because doing so will contribute to her own flourishing. If she believes this theory and is motivated by its claims about the source of her reasons, her primary impetus for acting rightly will be a desire for her own flourishing. But this egoistic motivation is inconsistent with genuine virtue, which is not focused primarily on the self.

Virtue ethicists, Toner contends, are not terribly troubled by this. Julia Annas (1993, 260), for example, regards the self-centeredness of an agent acting for the sake of her own flourishing as having concern "for oneself as a rational agent aiming at the fine."[35] Toner includes this as part of what he calls the 'complacent position': the view held by various Aristotelians that Aristotle's eudaimonistic ethics is indeed egoistic, but not in a troubling way.[36]

Why is this form of egoism not troubling? It is not worrying because it is what Toner calls 'formal foundational egoism.' He attributes this view to Rosalind Hursthouse in *On Virtue Ethics* (1999). He explains that, according to this perspective, a person's recognition that virtues benefit her is part of a larger ethical outlook, within which "the agent's good is no longer so narrowly conceived – that is, it can now include the good of others even at the foundational level" (Toner 2010, 285).

Yet some philosophers do find this form of egoism problematic. Toner (2006, 603–604) discusses two objections by John Hare (2001) to eudaimonism that bear on the topic. As Toner (2006, 603; emphasis his) describes the first objection, it is the claim that "even though eudaimonism acknowledges the claims of others in some sense, it does not recognize the claims of others *as other*, but only as related to the agent via similarity or affinity." Hare's second objection gets closer to the heart of the matter. He contends (2001, 37): "To make happiness central is to insist on the primacy of the relation of others to the self over what those others are in themselves, independently of the self, and this is unacceptably self-regarding."

---

[34] Quoted at Toner (2006), 599.   [35] Quoted at Toner (2006), 602.

[36] He believes that Annas and Terence Irwin, among others, hold this view (see Toner [2010, 276–277; 289–290]). Richard Kraut (1989, chapter 2), by contrast, argues that Aristotle's theory is not egoist at all.

Toner (2006, 603) glosses this by saying that "even though eudaimonism allows the agent to be concerned with the happiness of others, it does so through the device of making that happiness partly constitutive of the agent's own happiness, so that her attachments to others and their good is secondary."

The upshot is that the only way that the happiness of others can be part of my own is by being secondary to it. That is the only way, Hare thinks, that we can have a genuine case of self-love. However, making others' happiness conditional on my own is egoistic and ethically inadmissible. The primacy of self-love and true other-regard simply cannot coexist.

Annas (1988, 1–2) has a nice way of responding to this that is based on Aristotle's remarks, in *Nicomachean Ethics*, IX.8 in which Aristotle discusses the notion that the friend of virtue is "another self." Summarizing Aristotle, she writes (1988, 1):

> A friend, then, is one who (1) wishes and does good (or apparently good) things to a friend, for the friend's sake, (2) wishes the friend to exist and live, for his own sake, (3) spends time with his friend, (4) makes the same choices as his friend and (5) finds the same things pleasant and painful as his friend. But, argues Aristotle, all these marks are found paradigmatically in the good person's relation to himself.

According to Annas (1988, 1), one treats one's friend as one treats oneself. She quotes Aristotle: "Each of these seems to belong to the good person by virtue of his relation to himself, and he relates to his friend as he does to himself, for a friend is another self (1166 a 30–32)."

Annas (1988, 1–2) argues that Aristotle is not deriving friendship from self-love or giving an argument with self-love in the premises and friendship in the conclusion, but is instead, treating self-love as psychologically primary. As I read her argument, she is attributing to Aristotle a very sensible position, for where else could one start in forming friendships of virtue with others, if not from the basis of one's own virtuous attitudes toward oneself? It is not clear that the psychological primacy of self-love entails its moral primacy, as Hare (2001) seems to assume. By this I mean that psychological primacy is our natural starting point in our virtuous relations with others, but this does not entail that I must consider their good as secondary to and contingent upon its relation to my own. It is compatible with the psychological primacy of self-love in Aristotle's sense that I can view another's good as of equal moral importance with mine, as morally inseparable from mine, or even as having moral primacy over mine. In these kinds of cases, psychological self-love would not prohibit me from sacrificing my own good for that of another. In the last case, psychological self-love might even require it.

Two further points merit mention. First, Aristotle acknowledges good self-love and bad self-love.[37] Good self-love is felt for ourselves as the bearers of the higher rational capacities that enable us to be virtuous; bad self-love occurs when we extol and indulge baser desires and tendencies. Thus, what is best and finest in ourselves is what we wish for our friends, for their own sakes. It is true that having friends of virtue is part of our own happiness, but that is not why we wish them well for their own sake. We wish them well, in my view, because, as virtuous people, we want to see virtue extended and amplified. Good self-love provides the psychological outlook and attitudes from which we are able to do this.

Second, there are times when having friends of virtue will not contribute to our own flourishing. As Aristotle (*Nicomachean Ethics* 1171a21–b25) says, friends must stick together, in good fortune and bad. The good person must avoid causing his friends pain, should share his good fortune with them, and should give them due consideration in both their good and bad times. Sticking with our friends during their bad times might not contribute to our happiness, yet we are enjoined to do so for their sake. Is this enough to show that friendships of virtue – an essential part of one's flourishing for Aristotle – are not conditional upon their contributing to one's own happiness? If we are satisfied with the account thus far, we have reason to believe the charge of egoism has been adequately answered – either by Aristotle's view being considered egoistic in a benign and untroubling sense, or by its not being thought egoistic at all.

Other passages from Aristotle invite further consideration of the egoism objection, but delving into them would take us even deeper into the complexities of Aristotelian textual scholarship. Suffice it to say that the egoism or self-centeredness objection continues to be debated.

To the best of my knowledge, deliberations about the egoism or self-centeredness objection have taken place wholly within philosophy. The next objection to be considered, however, has spanned psychology as well as philosophy.

3.2 The Situationist Challenge: The First and Second Waves

The situationist challenge to virtue ethics was launched in two waves: the first wave focused on global traits, and the second, on the cognitive processes that integrate cohesive characters. Both waves have similar structures. In the first wave, some philosophers, making use of empirical studies in psychology, used

---

[37] See Annas (1988, 6) and, for example, Richard Kraut (1989, chapter 2) and Marcia Homiak (1981). Aristotle's discussion of good and bad self-love occurs in the *Nicomachean Ethics* at 1168b10–1169a15.

them to attack the idea that there can be virtues. In the second, the same philosophers shifted the focus of their attack to the idea that rational processes are sufficiently united to produce unified characters. Both waves make use of a tactic that I call the 'argument by overwhelming' – situationists amass dozens of empirical studies to support their positions, and, if any one or even several of those experiments are flawed, they claim that others are waiting in the wings to support their view. This in itself is problematic, but there are other problems with situationism, as we will see.

3.2.1 The First Wave

The first wave initially arose in the late twentieth and early twenty-first centuries. Drawing on troves of studies in social psychology, philosophers such as Gilbert Harman (1999, 2000, 2003), John M. Doris (1998, 2002), and Maria Merritt (2000) challenged the empirical adequacy of the moral psychology presupposed by Aristotelian virtue ethics. Their claim centered on global traits, which are understood as traits that are implicated in producing cross-situationally consistent behavior. What is cross-situationally consistent behavior? If someone has the trait of honesty, for example, she is expected to be honest in many different kinds of situations – when under oath in court, when conversing with her spouse, or when filing her income tax returns. Situationists take different positions on global traits. Harman (1999, 316; 2000, 223) contends that studies in social psychology give us little reason to believe that global traits exist. Doris (2002, 6) believes the studies indicate that global traits exist, but in such scarcity that they have little, if anything, to do with producing behavior. This, of course, has direct implications for virtue ethics, insofar as versions of it assume that virtues are indeed global traits. If such traits do not exist or have little impact on behavior, then we cannot become the kinds of people that virtue ethics tells us we should be (see Doris 2002, 6).

Responses to the challenge have been mixed. Some philosophers, such as Mark Alfano (2013), embrace the critique and seek to extend it to virtue epistemology. Others, such as Julia Annas (2005), Rachana Kamtekar (2004), and Gopal Sreenivasan (2002), argue against situationism on mainly philosophical grounds. Still others, such as Daniel C. Russell (2009) and Nancy Snow (2010), critique situationist arguments but also look to the CAPS (cognitive-affective processing system) theory, developed by psychologists Walter Mischel and Yuichi Shoda, as a way of finding an empirical grounding for Aristotelian-type virtues. In our forthcoming book, my colleagues in psychology Jennifer Cole Wright, Michael T. Warren, and I contend that Whole Trait Theory, a social-cognitivist psychological theory, provides a better empirical framework than the CAPS account for conceptualizing virtues as empirically measurable traits.[38] Finally, Christian Miller (2018, 2014, 2013) also looks to empirical psychology to generate explanations of character and behavior, advancing the view that our characters are comprised of 'mixed traits,' which are neither traditional virtues nor vices.

The gist of my response to situationism in *Virtue as Social Intelligence: An Empirically Grounded Theory* (2010, especially chapter 1) is that the situationist critique can be broken down into two claims: (1) that situations have profound effects on behavior; and (2) that claim (1) shows there is little or no room for the influence of global traits on behavior. We can accept the truth of (1), which is supported by abundant empirical evidence, without thereby also accepting (2). We need not accept (2) because philosophical situationists look to the wrong kinds of studies to support it – this is one of the problems with situationism to which I alluded earlier. For situationists such as Doris (2002), behavioral responses are indexed to objectively describable features of situations. Thus, Doris (2002, 25, 62ff; 1998, 507) endorses 'local' traits attributed on the basis of behavioral regularities observed to correlate with narrowly situation-specific features, such as 'answer-key' honesty, that is, being honest only when one has the chance to peek at an answer key to an exam but foregoes it, as opposed to 'finding change' honesty, which tracks one's honesty only when resisting the opportunity to pocket lost change. He does not endorse global traits because of his belief that cross-situationally consistent behavior cannot be empirically verified.

However, there is a body of empirical evidence from CAPS research that seems to belie this belief. (Doris [2002] argues against the importance of this evidence – to my mind, unconvincingly – for understanding moral character.) Proponents of CAPS found that how persons construe situations affects their behavior. Studies of children at a summer camp showed patterns of cross-situationally consistent behavior that were not indexed to objectively describable features of situations, but instead, to how subjects construed the situations, that is, to the psychological meanings they attributed to them. This led CAPS researchers to chart individual behavioral profiles, which took the form of "if, then" predictions, for example, 'If Johnny perceives he is being teased, then he is likely to behave aggressively,' or, 'If Amanda perceives she is being

---

[38] Colleagues in psychology, including my coauthor, Jennifer Cole Wright, persuaded me to make this change. For articulations of Whole Trait Theory (WTT), see Fleeson and Gallagher (2009), Fleeson and Jayawickreme (2015), and Jayawickreme and Fleeson (2017). On social-cognitivist psychology, I write: "Social-cognitivists conceptualize personality functioning in terms of the interactions of multiple cognitive and affective processes. These processes, they believe, develop in social and cultural contexts and are activated in social settings" Snow (2010, 19). See also Cervone and Shoda (1999, 4). WTT, like CAPS, is social-cognitivist.

threatened, then she is likely to behave fearfully.' The aggressive or fearful behavior depended on the child's perceiving the situation as inclusive of teasing or a threat. Aggressive or fearful behavior was likely to follow, whether the perceived teasing or threat occurred on the softball diamond, in woodworking class, while canoeing, or so on. The overall message is that subjects' perceptions of situations, and not necessarily the objectively describable features of situations, are essential to ascribing traits to people and to understanding trait-related behavior. This, of course, is highly compatible with the role that perception and practical wisdom play in understanding the actions of virtuous persons. Because of the CAPS theory's sensitivity to the importance of construal or perception, I argue that it is plausible to think of virtues as subsets of CAPS traits. An important proviso should be noted, however. For the psychologists who pioneered CAPS, CAPS traits are indexed to the psychological meanings that specific kinds of situations have for people. The proponents of CAPS rely exclusively on the data generated in their studies and do not claim that CAPS traits are or can be global. In my book (Snow 2010), I take the further step and argue that the meanings that situations have for people can be generalized across situation-types, both deliberately and nonconsciously. In other words, CAPS traits are capable of becoming global traits, even though Mischel and Shoda do not argue for that claim. I supply that argumentation in my book (Snow 2010). I do not know whether Mischel and Shoda would agree with my approach, but it is essential if CAPS is to provide a useful empirical framework for thinking about virtues as global traits.

My conception of virtue is meant to be ecumenical in the sense that it is inspired by Aristotle's conception, and is broadly compatible with more recent conceptions of virtue that are also indebted to his outlook. Thus, I believe that virtues are entrenched dispositions to act and respond emotionally, across different situation-types, in ways that are guided by practical wisdom and are appropriately motivated. Unlike Aristotle and some other views of virtue inspired by his conception, I argue that motivations have a unique role in unifying virtues qua traits: the motivations that are characteristic of specific virtues influence the cognitions, desires, and other elements that comprise the virtue such that, were the motivations removed or otherwise changed, the other elements would also change. This role for motivations is needed in order to distinguish virtues, as tightly unified bundles of cognitive and affective elements, from other kinds of CAPS traits, which do not incorporate the motivations characteristic of specific virtues, such as the desire to help another in need (characteristic of compassion) or the desire to tell the truth for its own sake (characteristic of honesty).

After making the case for virtues as a possible subset of CAPS traits, I review the main studies on which situationism relies in the last chapter of *Virtue as Social Intelligence* (Snow 2010). Like other critics of situationism, I do not find that the results of these studies, examined in their own right apart from the research that supports CAPS, give us reason to abandon hope in the existence or importance of global traits. Thus, they do not cast doubt on virtue ethics. In reviewing the studies, I found the psychologists who author them to be, in general, more cautious in their conclusions than the situationists who use them to critique virtue ethics. The upshot is that we can agree with situationists that situations profoundly influence behavior, yet maintain, contra situationism, that how people construe situations is key to finding empirical evidence of the kinds of traits that influence behavior.[39]

Let us return to the problems with situationism to which I referred earlier. One problem is that situationists look selectively to scientific studies to support their views. Other areas of psychology, for example, work on CAPS, are more amenable to the possibility of virtue than the studies that situationists adduce. The second issue is what I have called the 'argument by overwhelming.' In response to arguments that the specific studies they discuss do not truly support the claims they wish to make, situationists typically reply that many more studies do indeed support their claims. There is only way to decide the matter, and that is by a careful review of all of the studies that situationists adduce to support their contentions. I have not undertaken such a review, but I have read enough psychology and interacted with numerous psychologists who believe the situationist critique is mistaken. These experiences lead me to believe that the first wave of situationism misses its mark. As we will see in the next section, the same two problems bedevil the second wave of the situationist challenge.

3.2.2 The Second Wave

The second situationist challenge – what I call the 'second wave' – attacks the notion that practical rationality can integrate the various types of cognitive functioning of which people are capable. The seeds of the second wave were, I believe, planted during the first wave, in Doris' (2002) assertion that personality is 'evaluatively fragmented,' that is, that we do not have coherent characters or personalities in which traits nicely align and mesh well with each other. In other words, our characters are not made up of traits that are all either positively or negatively valenced. It is typically true that no one is all good or all bad; we are all somewhat mixed. Philosophers such as Kamtekar (2004)

---

[39] For a more recent overview of the first wave of the situationist challenge, see Bates and Kleingeld (2018).

pushed back on situationist claims about the fragmentation of personality, contending that practical rationality is capable of integrating our characters.

In a more recent article, however, Merritt, Doris, and Harman (2010) give the notion that our characters are fragmented a different and deeper twist.[40] Amassing a wealth of empirical evidence (here again, the 'argument by overwhelming'), they argue that practical reasoning itself is fragmented, and consequently, unable to sustain the cohesiveness of character required by virtue ethics. They do this by invoking dual-process theory in psychology, according to which our cognitive processing is of two types: controlled – deliberate and subject to conscious awareness – and automatic or outside of conscious awareness. My decision to take a break from writing and take a walk is deliberate and controlled; I am aware that I am making that decision. By contrast, because I have typed for many years, as I type these words, my finger motions are automatic. I do not have to pause and tell myself, "now position your left pinky finger over the 'a' key and press down"; I simply do so automatically, without conscious awareness or deliberation.

The gist of the situationist critique is that these processes can be at odds, as exhibited in a phenomenon they call 'moral dissociation' (Merritt, Doris, and Harman 2010, 367–370). This phenomenon, which they attribute to 'depersonalized response tendencies,' occurs when automatically produced behavior is at odds with normative commitments. The authors adduce a number of automaticity studies, mainly showing the effects of priming on behavior. 'Priming' occurs when participants in a psychological experiment nonconsciously pick up on cues that subsequently influence their behavior in ways of which they are not consciously aware. For example, in one word-scrambling study, research participants who had been placed in an "elderly" test condition were primed with words meant to elicit stereotypes, such as 'old,' 'lonely,' 'wrinkled,' and 'bingo.' They were subsequently observed to walk more slowly to an elevator than others in a control condition who had not been primed with such words. When participants in the "elderly" condition were asked if they had noticed the word primes, they replied that they had not, nor did they report noticing any effects on their subsequent behavior (see Merritt, Doris, and Harman 2010, 374).[41] The authors also call this phenomenon 'incongruency,' and note that it is

---

[40] See also Doris (2009), and my commentary on Merritt, Doris, and Harman (2010) in Snow (2013).

[41] The word-scrambling study cited by Merritt, Doris, and Harman (2010, 374) was one of a series of experiments done by Bargh, Chen, and Burrows (1996). That study has come under fire in the 'replicability crisis' that has affected psychological and other sciences. Studies in science are typically given credibility through replication – when attempts to repeat the studies yield the same or similar results. Many well-known and widely respected studies in psychology have recently failed that test. For example, Marjan Bakker et al. (2013, 120) contend that the study by

illustrated by other studies on stereotyping: we can have aversive reactions based on race, gender, and other factors which we would disavow and condemn were we aware of them. The authors write: "To the extent that automaticity is pervasive, it renders the virtue-ethical model of practical rationality problematic. Most obviously, incongruency unsettles notions of well-integrated deliberation."[42]

The authors soften their stance in the last section of their article, entitled "Remedial Measures," by noting studies within the automaticity literature on self-regulation and self-control and studies on interpersonal influences on moral cognition, which might contribute to agendas for deliberate self-improvement (Merritt, Doris, and Harman 2010, 378ff). That said, they are skeptical about the overall effectiveness of such strategies. If their view is correct, practical reasoning will likely not be able to integrate conscious and nonconscious processing to the extent needed for the unified moral character prescribed by virtue ethics.

As I argued in a review of their work, their view neglects three lines of research that suggest greater unity between conscious and nonconscious cognitive processes.[43] The first is studies of goal-dependent automaticity, which provide evidence that features of situations can nonconsciously activate representations of consciously chosen goals, thereby resulting in behavior that is conducive to goal pursuit. For example, psychologists conducted a study that showed that people exposed to a delicious-looking piece of chocolate cake did not succumb to temptation; instead, the researchers hypothesized that seeing the cake activated participants' goal to lose weight (see Fishbach, Friedman, and Kruglanski 2003). Such studies indicate greater harmony between conscious and nonconscious processes than Merritt, Doris, and Harman (2010) recognize. Secondly, the psychologists Daniel K. Lapsley and Patrick Hill (2008) offer a cognitive account of moral personality in which moral schemas – generalized knowledge structures which organize a person's moral beliefs, values, and so on – become chronically accessible and primed by environmental cues in ways that approach automaticity. For example, if I have in mind the schema of 'kind person' or 'good friend' as part of my self-conception, that is likely to nonconsciously influence my responses in various situations. When presented with appropriate cues, I will be more likely to help someone in need or comfort

---

Bargh, Chen, and Burrows (1996) has been cited over 2,000 times and included in social psychology textbooks, yet only two relatively direct but underpowered attempts at replication have been performed, both yielding inconclusive results. Any philosopher whose work relies on empirical psychological studies must be mindful of the implications of the replicability crisis for their views.

[42] See Merritt, Doris, and Harman (2010, 375); quoted at Snow (2013, 351).

[43] See Snow (2013, 351–353).

a friend than I would have been without those schemas. Moral schemas, like moral goals, are products of rational processes, and when primed, show how conscious and nonconscious processing can work together to unify moral personality. Finally, neuroscientific imaging studies of the brain suggest that a confederation of different systems supports brain functioning. Generally, the systems cooperate, though disagreements between beliefs and behavior reflect competition among systems. This research suggests underlying neural mechanisms by means of which cooperation, in addition to conflict, can be supported and explained. All three lines of research suggest greater harmony among conscious and nonconscious cognitive processing than Merritt, Doris, and Harman (2010) allow. In addition, Edward Slingerland (2011)'s discussion of the early Confucian use of situations to cultivate virtuous dispositions indicates that virtues need not be mere correctives to wayward nonconscious processes, but instead, have vital roles to play in shaping and unifying conscious as well as nonconscious processes.

To conclude, let us return to the 'argument by overwhelming.' My use of CAPS research to respond to the first wave of situationism, and the three lines of research I adduce to combat its second wave – studies of goal-dependent automaticity, of the use of moral schemas, and of neuroscientific imaging of the brain – suggest that the studies used in the 'arguments by overwhelming' are selected to advance situationist agendas. There are many other areas of research in psychology and in neuroscience that offer more positive pictures of our capacities for integrated characters and for acquiring and sustaining virtues, regarded as global traits.

3.3 Conclusion

The two objections considered here have importance beyond the present discussion. The egoism debate is still a live one, and situationist objections to virtue ethics have launched a new area of virtue study at the intersection of philosophy and psychology. Vigorous work by philosophers and psychologists, collaboratively as well as independently, has been underway for several years and shows no sign of abating (see Kristjánsson 2018b for an overview).

Concluding Comments

This volume has furnished a brief overview of recent work in neo-Aristotelian virtue ethics, as well as of alternative approaches to virtue. It has also provided a glimpse into two important objections to virtue ethics: the egoism or self-centeredness objection and situationist challenges. As I mentioned at the outset, many other perspectives on virtue have been omitted, as have other key challenges to virtue ethics. The burgeoning field of applied virtue ethics, which includes such timely areas as environmental virtue ethics and sexual virtue ethics, is also missing from this discussion.[44]

As the wealth of material on contemporary virtue ethics, including the publication of four new books on virtue in 2018 and one in 2019, attests, fascination with virtue persists.[45] Lively exploration of this interesting topic is more than likely to continue.

---

[44] The interested reader is advised to consult the essays in Snow (2018a) for further information.

[45] Bommarito (2018), Brady (2018), Kristjánsson (2018a), Stichter (2018), and McMullin (2019).

References

Adams, Robert M. 1999. *Finite and Infinite Goods: A Framework for Ethics*. New York, NY: Oxford University Press.

Adams, Robert M. 2006. *A Theory of Virtue: Excellence in Being for the Good*. Oxford, UK: Oxford University Press.

Alfano, Mark. 2013. *Character as Moral Fiction*. Cambridge, UK: Cambridge University Press.

Andreou, C. 2006. "Getting on in a Varied World." *Social Theory and Practice* 32(1): 61–73.

Angle, Stephen. 2009. *Sagehood: The Contemporary Significance of Neo-Confucian Philosophy*. New York: Oxford University Press.

Annas, Julia. 1988. "Self-Love in Aristotle." *The Southern Journal of Philosophy* 27 (supplement): 1–18.

Annas, Julia. 1992. "The Good Life and the Good Lives of Others." *Social Philosophy & Policy* 9(2): 133–148.

Annas, Julia. 1993. *The Morality of Happiness*. New York, NY: Oxford University Press.

Annas, Julia. 2005. "Comments on John Doris's *Lack of Character*." *Philosophy and Phenomenological Research* LXXI(3): 636–642.

Annas, Julia. 2011. *Intelligent Virtue*. Oxford, UK: Oxford University Press.

Annas, Julia. 2014. "Why Virtue Ethics Does Not Have a Problem with Right Action," in Mark Timmons, ed., *Oxford Studies in Normative Ethics*, vol. 4. Oxford, UK: Oxford University Press, 13–33.

Anscombe, G. E. M. 1958. "Modern Moral Philosophy." *Philosophy* 33(124): 1–16.

Aristotle. 1985. *The Nicomachean Ethics*. Trans. Terence Irwin. Indianapolis, IN: Hackett Publishing Company.

Aristotle. 2004. *The Eudemian Ethics*. Trans. H. Rackham. Loeb Classical Library, vol. XX, 2nd (revised) ed. Cambridge, MA: Harvard University Press.

Athanassoulis, Nafsika. 2018. "Acquiring Aristotelian Virtue," in Nancy E. Snow, ed., *The Oxford Handbook of Virtue*. New York, NY: Oxford University Press, 415–431.

Austin, Michael W. 2018. *Humility and Human Flourishing: A Study in Analytic Moral Theology*. New York, NY: Oxford University Press.

Badhwar, Neera K. 1996. "The Limited Unity of Virtue." *Noûs* 30(3): 306–329.

Bakker, Marjan, Cramer, Angélique O. J., Matzke, Dora, et al. 2013. "Open Peer Commentary: Dwelling on the Past." *European Journal of Personality* 27: 120–144.

Bargh, John A., Chen, Mark, and Burrows, Lara. 1996. "Automaticity of Social Behavior: Direct Effects of Trait Construct and Stereotype Activation on Action." *Journal of Personality and Social Behavior* 71(2): 230–244.

Baril, Anne. 2014. "Eudaimonia in Contemporary Virtue Ethics," in Stan van Hooft, ed., *The Handbook of Virtue Ethics*. Durham, UK: Acumen, 17–27.

Bates, Tom and Kleingeld, Pauline. 2018. "Virtue, Vice, and Situationism," in Nancy E. Snow, ed., *The Oxford Handbook of Virtue*. New York, NY: Oxford University Press, 524–545.

Bell, Macalester. 2006. "Review of Lisa Tessman's Burdened Virtues: Virtue Ethics for Liberatory Struggle." *Notre Dame Philosophical Review*. https://ndpr.nd.edu/news/25046-burdened-virtues-virtue-ethics-for-liberatory-strugles/.

Besser-Jones, Lorraine. 2014. *Eudaimonic Ethics: The Philosophy and Psychology of Living Well*. New York, NY: Routledge.

Bommarito, Nicholas. 2018. *Inner Virtue*. New York, NY: Oxford University Press.

Brady, Michael S. 2018. *Suffering and Virtue*. New York, NY: Oxford University Press.

Bucar, Elizabeth M. 2018. "Islamic Ethics," in Nancy E. Snow, ed., *The Oxford Handbook of Virtue*. New York,NY: Oxford University Press, 206–223.

Burnyeat, Myles. 1980. "Aristotle on Learning to Be Good," in A. O. Rorty, ed., *Essays on Aristotle's Ethics*. Berkeley, CA: University of California Press, 69–92.

Calhoun, Cheshire. 2008. "Reflections on the Metavirtue of Sensitivity to Suffering." *Hypatia* 23: 182–188.

Cervone, Daniel, and Shoda, Yuichi, eds. 1999. *The Coherence of Personality: Social-Cognitive Bases of Consistency, Variability, and Organization*. New York, NY: Guilford.

Chappell, Sophie-Grace. 2017. *Knowing What To Do: Imagination, Virtue, and Platonism in Ethics*. Oxford, UK: Oxford University Press.

Copp, D., and Sobel, D. 2004. "Morality and Virtue: An Assessment of Some Recent Work in Virtue Ethics." *Ethics* 114: 514–554.

Curzer, Howard J. 2002. "Aristotle's Painful Path to Virtue." *Journal of the History of Philosophy* 40(2): 141–162.

Curzer, Howard J. 2012. *Aristotle and the Virtues*. Oxford, UK: Oxford University Press.

Das, Ramon. 2003. "Virtue Ethics and Right Action." *Australasian Journal of Philosophy* 81(3): 324–339.

Dillon, Robin S. 2018. "Feminist Approaches to Virtue Ethics," in Nancy E. Snow, ed., *The Oxford Handbook of Virtue*. New York, NY: Oxford University Press, 377–397.

Doris, John M. 1998. "Persons, Situations, and Virtue Ethics." *Noûs* 32: 504–530.

Doris, John M. 2002. *Lack of Character: Personality and Moral Behavior.* Cambridge, UK: Cambridge University Press.

Doris, John M. 2009. "Skepticism about Persons." *Philosophical Issues* 19: 57–91.

Driver, Julia. 2001. *Uneasy Virtue.* Cambridge, UK: Cambridge University Press.

Dunnington, Kent. 2019. *Humility, Pride, and Christian Faith.* New York, NY: Oxford University Press.

Fishbach, Aylet, Friedman, Ronald S., and Kruglanski, Arie W. 2003. "Leading Us Not Unto Temptation: Momentary Allurements Elicit Overriding Goal Activation." *Journal of Personality and Social Psychology* 84(2): 296–309.

FitzPatrick, W. J. 2000. *Teleology and the Norms of Nature.* New York, NY: Garland Publishing.

Flanagan, Owen. 1991. *Varieties of Moral Personality: Ethics and Psychological Realism.* Cambridge, MA: Harvard University Press.

Flanagan, Owen. 2011. *The Bodhisattva's Brain: Buddhism Naturalized.* Cambridge, MA: The MIT Press.

Fleeson, W., and Gallagher, P. 2009. "The Implications of Big Five Standing for the Distribution of Trait Manifestation in Behavior: Fifteen Experience-Sampling studies and a Meta-Analysis." *Journal of Personality and Social Psychology* 97(6): 1097–1114.

Fleeson, W., and Jayawickreme, E. 2015. "Whole Trait Theory." *Journal of Research in Personality* 56: 82–92.

Foot, Philippa. 1978. *Virtues and Vices and Other Essays in Moral Philosophy.* Berkeley and Los Angeles, CA: University of California Press.

Foot, Philippa. 2001. *Natural Goodness.* Oxford, UK: Oxford University Press.

Foot, Philippa. 2002. "Does Moral Subjectivism Rest on a Mistake?" in Philippa Foot, *Moral Dilemmas and Other Topics in Philosophy*. Oxford, UK: Clarendon Press, 189–208.

Friedman, Marilyn. 2009. "Feminist Virtue Ethics, Happiness, and Moral Luck." *Hypatia* 24: 29–40.

Geach, Peter. 1977. *The Virtues.* Cambridge, UK: Cambridge University Press.

Greco,John. 2010. *Achieving Knowledge: A Virtue-Theoretic Account of Epistemic Normativity.* Cambridge, UK: Cambridge University Press.

Hare, John. 2001. "Scotus on Morality and Nature." *Medieval Philosophy and Theology* 9: 15–38.

Harman, Gilbert. 1999. "Moral Philosophy Meets Social Psychology: Virtue Ethics and the Fundamental Attribution Error." *Proceedings of the Aristotelian Society* 99: 315–331.

Harman, Gilbert. 2000. "The Nonexistence of Character Traits." *Proceedings of the Aristotelian Society* 100: 223–226.

Harman, Gilbert. 2003. "No Character or Personality." *Business Ethics Quarterly* 13: 87–94.

Homiak, Marcia L. 1981. "Virtue and Self-Love in Aristotle's Ethics." *Canadian Journal of Philosophy* 11(4): 633–651.

Hurka, Thomas. 2001. *Virtue, Vice, and Value.* New York, NY: Oxford University Press.

Hursthouse, Rosalind. 1999. *On Virtue Ethics.* Oxford, UK: Oxford University Press.

Hursthouse, R. 2004. "On the Grounding of the Virtues in Human Nature." In J. Szaif and M. Lutz Bachmann, eds., *Was ist das fur den Menschen Gute? What Is Good for a Human Being?* Berlin, Germany: DeGruyter, 263–275.

Hursthouse, R. 2012. "Human Nature and Aristotelian Virtue Ethics." *Royal Institute of Philosophy Supplement* 70: 169–188.

Hursthouse, Rosalind and Pettigrove, Glen. 2018. "Virtue Ethics," in Edward N. Zalta, ed., *The Stanford Encyclopedia of Philosophy.* https://plato.stanford.edu/archives/win2018/entries/ethics-virtue/.

Irwin, Terence. 1988. *Aristotle's First Principles.* New York, NY: Oxford University Press.

Jayawickreme, Eranda and Blackie, Laura E. R. 2016. *Exploring the Psychological Benefits of Hardship: A Critical Reassessment of Posttraumatic Growth.* Cham, Switzerland: SpringerBriefs in Psychology.

Jayawickreme, E. and Fleeson, W. 2017. "Whole Trait Theory Can Explain Virtues," in W. Sinnott-Armstrong and Christian. B. Miller, eds., *Moral Psychology: Virtue and Character*, Vol. 5. Cambridge, MA: MIT Press, 121–129.

Johansson, Jens and Svensson, Frans. 2018. "Objections to Virtue Ethics," in Nancy E. Snow, ed., *The Oxford Handbook of Virtue.* New York, NY: Oxford University Press, 491–507.

Johnson, Robert N. 2003. "Virtue and Right." *Ethics* 113: 810–834.

Kagan, Shelly. 1998. *Normative Ethics.* Boulder, CO: Westview Press.

Kamtekar, Rachana. 2004. "Situationism and Virtue Ethics on the Content of our Character." *Ethics* 114: 458–491.

Kant, Immanuel. 1993. *Grounding for the Metaphysics of Morals*. Trans. Frederick Ellington, 3rd ed. Indianapolis, IN: Hackett Publishing Company.

Kawall, Jason. 2009. "Virtue Theory, Ideal Observers, and the Supererogatory." *Philosophical Studies* 146: 179–196.

Kraut, Richard. 1989. *Aristotle on the Human Good*. Princeton, NJ: Princeton University Press.

Kristjánsson, Kristján. 2015. *Aristotelian Character Education*. New York, NY: Routledge.

Kristjánsson, Kristján. 2018a. *Virtuous Emotions*. New York, NY: Oxford University Press.

Kristjánsson, Kristján. 2018b. "Virtue from the Perspective of Psychology," in Nancy E. Snow, ed., *The Oxford Handbook of Virtue*. New York, NY: Oxford University Press, 546–568.

Lapsley, Daniel K. and Hill, Patrick. 2008. "On Dual Processing and Heuristic Approaches to Moral Cognition." *Journal of Moral Education* 37(3): 322–323.

LeBar, Mark. 2013. *The Value of Living Well*. New York, NY: Oxford University Press.

LeBar, Mark. 2018. "Eudaimonism," in Nancy E. Snow, ed., *The Oxford Handbook of Virtue*. New York. NY: Oxford University Press, 470–487.

Lemos, John. 1994. "The Unity of the Virtues and Its Recent Defenses." *Southern Journal of Philosophy* 32(1): 85–106.

Lewens, T. 2010. "Foot Note." *Analysis* 70(3): 468–473.

Lewens, T. 2012. "Human Nature: The Very Idea." *Philosophy and Technology* 25(4): 459–474.

Lott, M. 2012. "Moral Virtue as Knowledge of Human Form." *Social Theory and Practice* 38(3): 407–431.

Louden, Robert B. 1984. "On Some Vices of Virtue Ethics." *American Philosophical Quarterly* 21(3): 227–236.

MacIntyre, Alasdair. 1984. *After Virtue: A Study in Moral Theory*, 2nd ed. Notre Dame, IN: The University of Notre Dame Press.

MacIntyre, Alasdair. 1999. *Dependent Rational Animals: Why Human Beings Need the Virtues*. Peru, IL: Carus Publishing Company.

MacIntyre, Alasdair. 2016. *Ethics in the Conflicts of Modernity: An Essay on Desire, Practical Reasoning, and Narrative*. Cambridge, UK: Cambridge University Press.

MacKenzie, Matthew. 2018. "Buddhism and the Virtues," in Nancy E. Snow, ed., *The Oxford Handbook of Virtue*. New York, NY: Oxford University Press, 153–170.

McDowell, John. 1979. "Virtue and Reason." *The Monist* 62(3): 331–350.

McDowell, John. 1998. "Two Sorts of Naturalism," in *Mind, Value, and Reality*. Cambridge, MA: Harvard University Press, 167–197.

McKerlie, Dennis. 1998. "Aristotle and Egoism." *The Southern Journal of Philosophy*. XXXVI: 531–555.

McMullin, Irene. 2019. *Existential Flourishing: A Phenomenology of the Virtues*. Cambridge, UK: Cambridge University Press.

Merritt, Maria. 2000. "Virtue Ethics and Situationist Personality Psychology." *Ethical Theory and Moral Practice* 3: 365–383.

Merritt, Maria, Doris, John M., and Harman, Gilbert. 2010. "Character," in John M. Doris and the Moral Psychology Research Group, eds., *The Moral Psychology Handbook*. Oxford, UK: Oxford University Press, 355–401.

Miller, Christian B. 2013. *Moral Character: An Empirical Theory*. Oxford, UK: Oxford University Press.

Miller, Christian B. 2014. *Character and Moral Psychology*. Oxford, UK: Oxford University Press.

Miller, Christian B. 2018. *The Character Gap: How Good Are We?* New York, NY: Oxford University Press.

Millgram, Elijah. 2009. Critical notice of Life and Action. *Analysis* 69(3): 557–564.

Moosavi, P. 2018. "Neo-Aristotelian Naturalism and the Evolutionary Objection: Rethinking the Relevance of Empirical Science." In J. Hacker-Wright, ed., *Philippa Foot on Goodness and Virtue*. Cham, Switzerland: Palgrave Macmillan, 277–308.

Nagel, Thomas. 1986. *The View from Nowhere*. Oxford, UK: Oxford University Press.

Nolan, Kirk J. 2014. *Reformed Virtue after Barth: Developing Moral Virtue Ethics in the Reformed Tradition*. Louisville, KY: Westminster John Knox Press.

Nussbaum, Martha C. 1988. "Non-Relative Virtues: An Aristotelian Approach." *Midwest Studies in Philosophy* 13(1): 32–53.

Odenbaugh, J. 2017. "Nothing in Ethics Makes Sense in the Light of Evolution? Natural Goodness, Normativity, and Naturalism." *Synthese* 194: 1031–1055.

Olberding, Amy. 2012. *Moral Exemplars in the Analects: The Good Person Is That*. New York, NY: Routledge Press.

Oliner, S. P., and Oliner, P. M. 1988. *The Altruistic Personality: Rescuers of Jews in Nazi Europe*. New York, NY: The Free Press.

Pettigrove, Glen. 2014. "Virtue Ethics, Virtue Theory, and Moral Theology," in Stan van Hooft, ed., *The Handbook of Virtue Ethics*. Durham, UK: Acumen, 88–104.

Pettigrove, Glen. 2018. "Alternatives to Neo-Aristotelian Virtue Ethics," in Nancy E. Snow, ed., *The Oxford Handbook of Virtue*. New York, NY: Oxford University Press, 259–376.

Prichard, H. A. 1995. "Does Moral Philosophy Rest on a Mistake?" in Steven Cahn and Joram Haber, eds., *Twentieth Century Ethical Theory*. Englewood Cliffs, NJ: Prentice-Hall, 37–47.

Riesbeck, David J. 2016. *Aristotle on Political Community*. Cambridge, UK: Cambridge University Press.

Robertson, Seth. 2019. "*Nunchi*, Ritual, and Early Confucian Ethics." *Dao* 18: 23–40.

Russell, Daniel C. 2009. *Practical Intelligence and the Virtues*. New York, NY: Oxford University Press.

Russell, Daniel C. 2012. *Happiness for Humans*. Oxford, UK: Oxford University Press.

Russell, Daniel C. 2014. "Phronesis and the Virtues (NE VI. 12–13)," in Ronald Polansky, ed., *The Cambridge Companion to Aristotle's Nicomachean Ethics*. New York, NY: Cambridge University Press, 203–220.

Russell, Daniel C. 2015. "Aristotle on Cultivating Virtue," in Nancy E. Snow, ed.,*Cultivating Virtue: Perspectives from Philosophy, Theology, and Psychology*. New York, NY: Oxford University Press, 17–48.

Sherman, Nancy. 2015. *Afterwar: Healing the Moral Wounds of Our Soldiers*. New York, NY: Oxford University Press.

Sim, May. 2007. *Remastering Morals with Aristotle and Confucius*. Cambridge, UK: Cambridge University Press.

Sim, May. 2018. "The Phronimos and the Sage," in Nancy E. Snow, ed., *The Oxford Handbook of Virtue*. New York, NY: Oxford University Press, 190–205.

Slingerland, Edward. 2011. "The Situationist Critique and Early Confucian Virtue Ethics." *Ethics* 121: 390–419.

Slote, Michael. 1992. *From Morality to Virtue*. Oxford, UK: Oxford University Press.

Slote, Michael. 1997. "Virtue Ethics," in Marcia Baron, Philip Pettit, and Michael Slote, eds., *Three Methods of Ethics*. Oxford, UK: Blackwell, 175–238.

Slote, Michael. 2001. *Morals from Motives*. New York, NY: Oxford University Press.

Slote, Michael. 2010. *Moral Sentimentalism*. New York, NY: Oxford University Press.

Slote, Michael. 2018. "Sentimentalist Virtue Ethics," in Nancy E. Snow, ed., *The Oxford Handbook of Virtue*. New York, NY: Oxford University Press, 343–358.

Snow, Nancy E. 2010. *Virtue as Social Intelligence: An Empirically Grounded Theory*. New York, NY: Routledge.

Snow, Nancy E. 2013. "'May You Live in Interesting Times': Moral Philosophy and Empirical Psychology." *Journal of Moral Philosophy* 10: 339–353.

Snow, Nancy E. 2015. "Comments on *Intelligent Virtue*: Outsmarting Situationism." *Journal of Value Inquiry* 49(1): 297–306.

Snow, Nancy E. (ed.). 2018a. *The Oxford Handbook of Virtue*. New York, NY: Oxford University Press.

Snow, Nancy E. 2018b. "Neo-Aristotelian Virtue Ethics," in Nancy E. Snow, ed., *The Oxford Handbook of Virtue*. New York, NY: Oxford University Press, 321–242.

Snow, Nancy E. 2018c. "From Ordinary Virtue to Aristotelian Virtue," in Tom Harrison and David Walker, eds., *The Theory and Practice of Virtue Education*.London, UK: Routledge, 67–81.

Snow, Nancy E. 2019. "Virtue Proliferation: A Clear and Present Danger?," in Elisa Grimi, ed., *Virtue Ethics: Retrospect and Prospect*. New York, NY: Springer, 177–196.

Solomon, David. 1988. "Internal Objections to Virtue Ethics." *Midwest Studies in Philosophy* 13(1): 428–441.

Sosa, Ernest. 2007. *A Virtue Epistemology: Apt Belief and Reflective Knowledge*, Vol. 1. Oxford, UK: Oxford University Press.

Sosa, Ernest. 2009. *A Virtue Epistemology: Apt Belief and Reflective Knowledge*, Vol. 2. Oxford, UK: Oxford University Press.

Sreenivasan, Gopal. 2002. "Errors about Errors: Virtue Theory and Trait Attribution." *Mind* 111(441): 47–68.

Stalnaker, Aaron. 2020. *Mastery, Dependence, and the Ethics of Authority*. New York, NY: Oxford University Press.

Stangl, Rebecca. 2018. "Cultural Relativity and Justification," in Nancy E. Snow, ed., *The Oxford Handbook of Virtue*. New York, NY: Oxford University Press, 508–523.

Stichter, Matt. 2018. *The Skillfulness of Virtue: Improving Our Moral and Epistemic Lives*. New York, NY: Cambridge University Press.

Swanton, Christine. 2003. *Virtue Ethics: A Pluralistic View*. Oxford, UK: Oxford University Press.

Swanton, Christine. 2015. *The Virtue Ethics of Hume and Nietzsche*. Oxford, UK: Wiley Blackwell.

Swanton, Christine. 2018. "Virtue in Hume and Nietzsche," in Nancy E. Snow, ed., *The Oxford Handbook of Virtue* . New York, NY: Oxford University Press, 241–262.

Tessman, Lisa. 2005. *Burdened Virtues: Virtue Ethics for Liberatory Struggles*. New York, NY: Oxford University Press.

Thompson, Michael. 1995. "The Representation of Life," in R. Hursthouse, G. Lawrence, and W. Quinn, eds., *Virtues and Reasons: Philippa Foot and Moral Theory*. Oxford, UK: Clarendon Press, 247–296.

Thompson, Michael. 2003. "Three Degrees of Natural Goodness." *Iride*. Online at: www.pitt.edu/~mthompso/: 1–7.

Thompson, Michael. 2004. "Apprehending Human Form," in Anthony O'Hear, ed., *Modern Moral Philosophy*. Cambridge, UK: Cambridge University Press, 47–74.

Thompson, Michael. 2008. *Life and Action: Elementary Structures of Practice and Practical Thought*. Cambridge, MA: Harvard University Press.

Thompson, Michael. 2013. "Forms of Nature," in G. Hindrichs and H. Axel, eds., *Freiheit*. Stuttgarter Hegel-Kongres, Frankfurt am Main: Vittorio Klostermann, 701–735.

Tiwald, Justin. 2018. "Confucianism and Neo-Confucianism," in Nancy E. Snow, ed., *The Oxford Handbook of Virtue*. New York, NY: Oxford University Press, 171–189.

Toner, Christopher. 2006. "The Self-Centredness Objection to Virtue Ethics." *Philosophy* 81(318): 595–617.

Toner, Christopher. 2008. "Sorts of Naturalism: Requirements for a Successful Theory." *Metaphilosophy* 39(2): 220–250.

Toner, Christopher. 2010. "Virtue Ethics and the Nature and Forms of Egoism." *Journal of Philosophical Research* 35: 275–303.

van Hooft, Stan. 2014. "Introduction," in Stan van Hooft, ed., *The Handbook of Virtue Ethics*. Durham, UK: Acumen, 1–14.

Vasilou, Iakovos. 1996. "The Role of Good Upbringing in Aristotle's Ethics." *Philosophy and Phenomenological Research* 56(4): 771–797.

Vogler, Candace. 2018. "Turning to Aquinas on Virtue," in Nancy E. Snow, ed., *The Oxford Handbook of Virtue*. New York, NY: Oxford University Press, 224–240.

Walker, L. J., & Frimer, J. A. 2007. "Moral Personality of Brave and Caring Exemplars." *Journal of Personality and Social Psychology* 93(5): 845-860.

Watson, Gary. 1984. "Virtues in Excess." *Philosophical Studies* 46(1): 57–74.

Watson, Gary. 1990. "The Primacy of Character," in Owen Flanagan and Amélie Oksenberg Rorty, eds., *Identity, Character, and Morality: Essays in Moral Psychology*. Cambridge, MA: The MIT Press, 449–469.

Watson, Gary. 2004. "Two Faces of Responsibility," in *Agency and Answerability: Selected Essays*. Oxford, UK: Oxford University Press, 260–288.

Williams, Bernard. 1985. *Ethics and the Limits of Philosophy.* London, UK: Fontana Press.

Wolf, Susan. 2007. "Moral Psychology and the Unity of the Virtues." *Ratio* (new series) XX(2): 145–167.

Wood, W. Jay. 2018. "Christian Theories of Virtue," in Nancy E. Snow, ed., *The Oxford Handbook of Virtue.* New York, NY: Oxford University Press, 281–300.

Woodcock, S. 2006. "Philippa Foot's Virtue Ethics Has an Achilles' Heel." *Dialogue* 45(6): 445–468.

Wright, Jennifer Cole, Warren, Michael, and Snow, Nancy E. (in press). *Understanding Virtue: Theory and Measurement.* New York, NY: Oxford University Press.

Zagzebski, Linda. 1996. *Virtues of the Mind: An Inquiry into the Nature of Virtue and the Ethical Foundations of Knowledge.* Cambridge, UK: Cambridge University Press.

Zagzebski, Linda. 2010. "Exemplarist Virtue Theory," in Heather Battaly, ed., *Virtue and Vice: Moral and Epistemic.* Malden, MA: Wiley-Blackwell, 39–55.

Zagzebski, Linda. 2017. *Exemplarist Moral Theory.* New York, NY: Oxford University Press.

Acknowledgments

I am grateful to Dale E. Miller, Ben Eggleston, and three anonymous reviewers for helpful comments on earlier versions of this volume.

Cambridge Elements ≡

Elements in Ethics

Ben Eggleston
University of Kansas

Ben Eggleston is a professor of philosophy at the University of Kansas. He is the editor of John Stuart Mill, *Utilitarianism: With Related Remarks from Mill's Other Writings* (Hackett, 2017) and a co-editor of *Moral Theory and Climate Change: Ethical Perspectives on a Warming Planet* (Routledge, 2020), *The Cambridge Companion to Utilitarianism* (Cambridge, 2014), and *John Stuart Mill and the Art of Life* (Oxford, 2011). He is also the author of numerous articles and book chapters on various topics in ethics.

Dale E. Miller
Old Dominion University, Virginia

Dale E. Miller is a professor of philosophy at Old Dominion University. He is the author of *John Stuart Mill: Moral, Social and Political Thought* (Polity, 2010) and a co-editor of *Moral Theory and Climate Change: Ethical Perspectives on a Warming Planet* (Routledge, 2020), *A Companion to Mill* (Blackwell, 2017), *The Cambridge Companion to Utilitarianism* (Cambridge, 2014), *John Stuart Mill and the Art of Life* (Oxford, 2011), and *Morality, Rules, and Consequences: A Critical Reader* (Edinburgh, 2000). He is also the editor-in-chief of *Utilitas*, and the author of numerous articles and book chapters on various topics in ethics broadly construed.

About the Series
This Elements series provides an extensive overview of major figures, theories, and concepts in the field of ethics. Each entry in the series acquaints students with the main aspects of its topic while articulating the author's distinctive viewpoint in a manner that will interest researchers.

Cambridge Elements ☰

Elements in Ethics

Elements in the Series

Utilitarianism
Tim Mulgan

Nietzsche's Ethics
Thomas Stern

Buddhist Ethics
Maria Heim

Contractualism
Jussi Suikkanen

Epistemology and Methodology in Ethics
Tristram McPherson

Ethical Subjectivism and Expressivism
Neil Sinclair

Moore's Ethics
William H. Shaw

Thomas Reid on the Ethical Life
Terence Cuneo

Contemporary Virtue Ethics
Nancy E. Snow

A full series listing is available at www.cambridge.org/EETH